AUTO REPAIR FRAUDS:

HOW TO PREVENT YOUR CAR FROM DRIVING YOU TO THE POORHOUSE

by **Monty Norris**
Produced by Lyle Kenyon Engel

ARCO PUBLISHING COMPANY INC.

219 Park Avenue South, New York, N.Y. 10003

Produced by Lyle Kenyon Engel

Text by Monty Norris

Editorial Staff
  George Engel
  Marla Ray

Published by Arco Publishing Company, Inc.
219 Park Avenue South, New York, N.Y. 10003

Library of Congress Catalog Card Number 74-32631
ISBN 0-668-03763-6

Printed in the United States of America

Contents

	Introduction	5
1	*Why Is the Auto-Repair Industry in Such a Mess?*	9
2	*How Good Is Your Mechanic?*	23
3	*Watch for These Common Frauds*	35
4	*How Good Is That Guarantee?*	49
5	*Where to Take a Sick Car*	63
6	*The Anatomy of an Automobile*	85
7	*Getting Along with Your Car*	125
8	*What to Do if You Get Gypped*	143
	Appendix 1: Where to Write for Help	159
	Appendix 2: An Automotive Dictionary	181
	Index	189

Introduction

It's the number-one consumer complaint in the country. Some law-enforcement officials and legislators say it's the nation's biggest con game. The subject? Auto repair.

Americans pay out more than $29 *billion* a year to service and repair more than 110 million automobiles, and yet, according to a three-year U.S. Senate subcommittee investigation into the auto-repair industry, a full one-third of all car-repair dollars—$10 billion a year—is wasted on inadequate, inept, or corrupt service. And that's not all. A diagnostic center, established under federal grant, found that 75 percent of all the cars it examined had at least one safety defect, and a California Highway Patrol investigation of 400 fatal accidents revealed that 29 percent of the cars involved were mechanically defective and that in most cases these defects caused or contributed to the accidents.

So who's to blame for the auto-repair mess? Does the problem begin at the factory with sloppy workmanship and poor quality control? What about auto dealerships that are more interested in selling a lot of cars than in satisfying customers or servicing the autos they have already sold? Or is the problem primarily crooked mechanics looking for a fast and easy buck? Each of these circumstances plays a part in the drama, but then so do most motorists who too often make themselves easy prey through ignorance and lazy consumer habits.

This book will explore the industry and explain how you can avoid being one of the growing number of victims of crooked or incompetent auto service. For example, did you know that incompetence isn't illegal in most states? Not in car repairs, at least. The mechanic who robs you on purpose can be prosecuted. The one who does it unwittingly can't. Sound ridiculous? You bet. But to the motorist stuck with a bill for unnecessary or shoddy work the results seem the same. And they are. In this book you'll find out how to avoid such frustrating situations and what to do if you are victimized.

We will also explore just how good that warranty is on your new or recycled car. It's probably a lot better than you think and certainly better than a good many service departments and auto dealers would like you to believe.

But where should you take an ailing car? That's the question most often asked by car owners. We'll give you a detailed look at six kinds of auto-repair shops and examine the good and bad in each: (1) new-car dealerships with attached service and parts departments; (2) large independent general repair shops; (3) garages franchised by national companies (and supported by very heavy advertising) which specialize in selling and installing the parent company's rebuilt engines, transmissions, brakes, or mufflers; (4) the small one- or two-man operations; (5) the several thousands of gas stations with their one or two service stalls; and (6) the modern diagnostic centers which, for a fee, will give your car a thorough physical examination designed to locate and identify any and all ailments.

How to cope with body repairs, insurance claims, repossessions, and other legal hassles is another subject that baffles and frustrates many car owners. This book will encourage motorists not to be intimidated by legal mumbo jumbo or pressured into accepting without question what giant corporations tell them. You can learn to be a tough customer—which usually means you wind up a more satisfied one. And that's the way it should be.

We will look into the sometimes agonizing question of determining just how much fixing (if any) your car really needs *before* you invest a lot of money. We will examine some of the most common tricks employed by crooked repairmen to bilk unwitting customers and offer tips on how to avoid them. How to take legal action if you are victimized will also be discussed.

But even if you are an expert on auto repair and good service, the secret of preventing your car from driving you to the poorhouse is regular maintenance and checkups. Prevention is still better than any cure. The majority of auto repairs can be prevented entirely if you learn and practice good automotive health habits. A little automotive preventive medicine like that described in this book, if followed with reasonable regularity, will have the same beneficial effect on your car that a good diet, regular exercise, and plenty of sleep will have on you.

Every trade and profession has its charlatans, and this one is no exception. The majority of mechanics, however, are honest, if not always competent. Yet there are admittedly more schlock operators in the auto-repair business than in almost any other. So you and I must become aware of the tricks these repair bandits employ, and we must learn how to spot incompetence. Unfortunately, it isn't always easy to tell the honest mechanic from the rip-off artist, much less the skilled from the blundering. That's why this book was written. Read it. Underline it. Keep it in your car, and refer to it frequently. It can save you money and prevent headaches.

Chapter 1

Why Is the Auto-Repair Industry in Such a Mess?

Every automobile on the road today began as an abstract idea in the mind of some designer, was then refined through executive discussion and the science of engineering, constructed through application of modern technology, and marketed via mass media by clever amateur psychologists in the advertising business. These master propagandists from Madison Avenue convince us that Detroit's products will offer us comfort, style, performance, excitement, prestige, high resale value, and even sexual gratification. Rarely, if ever, do they mention reliability and dependable service. Probably because they'd be laughed out of a job.

But the state of the automobile in America today is no laughing matter. Certainly not to the literally millions of motorists who every year waste billions of dollars on shabby or inept service on high-priced vehicles that could—and should—give them 75,000 to 100,000 miles of relatively trouble-free service. American car owners who can boast of complete satisfaction with both their automobile and repair work are rare indeed. They may even be a vanishing species.

The flaws in automobile service that seem to plague growing numbers of motorists are more than chance errors and occasional flubs in an otherwise sound system. They are, rather, built-in weaknesses in the entire industry—beginning on the Detroit drawing board and ending in your garage. To understand fully why automobiles seem to be so difficult and expensive to keep running, we have to start at the factory—right in the executive offices where policy is established.

One of these policies is planned obsolescence. American auto makers have long believed that in order to sell cars they have to give the public something new all the time, which means that every car is made obsolete every two or three years by the introduction of a new (but not necessarily *better*) version. Any engineer will tell you that the longer you build a machine the better it gets, simply because you can improve on its faults and weaknesses. In the two to three years after a new-model car is introduced, service departments around the country have fed enough information back to the factory for engineers there to learn what improvements and changes or modifications should be made to improve the product. Unfortunately, instead of using this information to refine cars, Detroit executives scrap the original design and start producing a new one. The cycle begins all over again.

Much of the favorable reputation foreign cars have enjoyed is based on manufacturer reluctance to make such abrupt changes. But, alas, with increased production and competition, even some of these stalwarts of reliability are having their problems.

Since cars are sold more by their aesthetic appeal than engineering quality, a great deal of emphasis, effort, time, money, and energy is spent in coming up with such design disasters as recessed windshield wipers, hidden headlights, and built-in bumpers that must be removed just to replace a ten-cent light bulb. All of these so-called "styling innovations" have tremendous appeal to car buyers in this country until they discover (too late) the expensive and inconvenient consequences of this unnecessary gadgetry.

Perhaps the most glaring example of styling blunder in recent history was the General Motors fiasco of 1975, when owners of that giant auto maker's sporty Chevrolet Monza, along with the Oldsmobile and Buick versions of the same model, discovered they couldn't install chains for winter driving because of the shape of the fender wells.

This is one of many outrageous examples of how designers and manufacturers sacrifice function for style. Not surprisingly, more than a few owners and mechanics were displeased with this ridiculous situation. Meanwhile, GM blushingly admitted it would have to make a few changes in what was "apparently an engineering oversight."

Next on the long list of problems is the assembly line where your car and mine is put together—largely by a chain of bored, disenchanted, and often poorly trained workers. It's a system that dehumanizes and breeds the kind of frustration that ultimately produces sloppy workmanship and often outright sabotage. Employee turnover in many auto plants is as high as 40 percent a year, according to U.S. Department of

Labor statistics, and absenteeism is the highest of any industry. I've talked with numerous auto assembly-line employees over the past few years who freely admitted they often showed up at work under the influence of drugs and alcohol and even regularly engaged in acts of sabotage, simply to relieve the endless boredom of their jobs.

It's little wonder then, even beyond the inherent design problems of so many cars, that doors won't close properly, windows won't seal, wiring short-circuits, and trunk compartments leak. These and a multitude of other irritating problems vividly point out sloppy work-manship and poor or ineffective quality control.

Yet, despite these serious weaknesses in the manufacture of automo-biles, American cars today are, on the whole, greatly superior to their ancestors—and certainly safer. Assuming regular maintenance is performed, modern engines and transmissions can and should last for around 75,000 to 100,000 miles without major repairs or overhaul. Brakes work better and last longer than ever before. Tires, if not abused, are almost failsafe. These are surely major safety factors in anybody's book.

Then why, you may ask, are there so many *little things* always going wrong with a $4000 or even $10,000 car that seems basically sound? The answer to that question is both simple and complicated. Much of the problem lies in the fact that today's cars are much more sophisticated (or complicated, perhaps) than the buggies of 20 or 30 years ago. A machine with 50,000 moving parts has a much greater chance of breaking down or needing some kind of adjustment from time to time than one with half that number.

Today's high-powered V8 engines and the more economical four- and six-cylinder powerplants are basically only refined versions of what was under the hood of some of the earliest horseless carriages. It's the window dressing like the previously described styling abortions, plus trimmings like power steering and brakes, smog devices, interlocking safety belt–ignition systems, hidden antennas, etc., that begin to complicate matters, increase the odds of failure, and make trouble-shooting more difficult.

Compound this situation with the fact that most American manufac-turers (and a growing number of foreign-car makers as well) rely on their dealerships across the country to catch booboos that should have been spotted and corrected before the car ever left the factory. This is supposed to be accomplished through the so-called "preparation charges," which the buyer pays for, and the warranty, under which the manufacturer assumes the cost. However, dealer preparation is often nothing more than a quick wash job. Few cars receive any expert attention.

For years now, I have made it a routine practice to go over every new car I've purchased, tightening and adjusting nuts and bolts and screws. I've also helped several friends and colleagues do the same. In more than two decades, I've yet to come across one automobile that didn't require more than what I consider a reasonable amount of tightening and adjusting. At the very least, such sloppy quality control eventually leads to the irritating rattles and squeaks that are so unnecessarily commonplace in many cars today.

Absurd? Indeed. Who's fault? Both manufacturer and dealer. Neither is taking the responsibility for making sure his product is ready for delivery. The manufacturer dumps the burden on the dealer, who in turn kisses it off, hoping the customers won't notice. And most don't, because they're too busy or preoccupied with color and optional equipment, or haggling over price, to give even a minute's thought to how sound their investment really is.

Nor do most new-car buyers ever test drive the product they are investing a lot of money and faith in until after signing a contract. They may drive a demonstration model to see how they like the car and then pick the color, equipment, and body style of that same make from a selection on the back lot or even the showroom floor. But that isn't the same thing as driving the car you plan on going home in. Not at all.

True, some dealers may balk at the idea of using anything except demo models for test driving, usually explaining that if a car is driven by a customer it can no longer be considered a "new" car. They'll probably say things like: "How would you like to buy a new car that already had two hundred miles on it? That's why we have demonstrators, to save our new-car selection for the buyers."

They'll smile rather condescendingly when they give that little speech. So you just smile right back with an air of bemused tolerance and say: "But if the car checks out, I'll buy it. And if it doesn't, then I'm doing you a favor, right? I mean, you wouldn't want to sell a customer a lemon. Would you?"

If that doesn't work, just smile and say you're afraid you'll have to shop elsewhere. And do. What determines a new car is ownership or registration—not mileage. But most buyers are as anxious to get the keys and drive off as the salespersons are to collect their commissions. As a result, few customers ever insist on driving the car they're actually buying.

A sloppy system, then, is encouraged and perpetuated by equally sloppy consumer habits. So, while auto makers and their dealers may well be remiss in some respects, the public hasn't done much to combat the situation. In fact, we've made it easy. But that still doesn't make it right, or unavoidable.

Next we have the new-car warranty. This has been described by many consumer crusaders and legal experts around the country as little more than a cruel hoax perpetrated on a gullible public. I'm inclined to agree, and we'll go into contracts and warranties at great length later. The truth is that most of us are better protected than we realize, but few of us ever exert our rights under the law, either out of ignorance or a lack of willingness to get tough and face up to a legal fight that can, and often does, drag out for months.

Few insiders will dispute the fact that there are two sets of standards at dealerships—one for warranty work and one for nonwarranty work. A dealer, faced with the low labor rate paid by a factory for warranty work, can be expected in a competitive business climate to favor nonwarranty repairs where he can charge the customer whatever he can get away with. The manufacturers' flat-rate system has become the norm throughout the industry. The quicker the mechanic works, then, the more money he and his bosses take in. Flat rates, as many mechanics have admitted to me, encourage parts changing rather than actual repair. It often takes much too long to repair something. It's easier for a mechanic to install a new or rebuilt part on your car than it is to take apart and fix whatever is broken. The profit margin is also often considerably greater.

I remember a few years ago when the fuel pump in my vintage transportation buggy went on the blink. I took it to two or three garages, and each of them wanted to install either a new or rebuilt fuel pump, charging me an hour's labor for the job. I finally decided to take the thing apart myself, find what was wrong, and fix it if at all possible. The trouble was a bad diaphragm. Had I let one of the garages do the job it would have cost me about $20. By contrast, it took me less than an hour and cost about $2, including the can of beer I drank while working. I use this example to show how often motorists pay for much more than they need and still don't get their money's worth. And I daresay you hardly have to be a master mechanic to remove and take apart a fuel pump! A little experienced, perhaps, but not especially skilled.

The number of instances where complaints have shown a dealer stalled on repairs in order to outwait the warranty period is also disturbingly high, according to Michael S. Kraft, Assistant Attorney

General of New York. Domestic manufacturers in the last two or three years have reduced the warranty coverage from 24 months or 24,000 miles to 12 months or 12,000 miles, whichever comes first. Even this shortened warranty can be jeopardized if you have outside repairs made, even though the warranty says this is permissible.

"The warranty as it really reads is not a warranty for consumers' protection," Kraft says. "It's a warranty for factory protection. It's a limiting statement; it's not an expansion of services."

Dealers aren't supposed to lose money on warranty work. But, according to the National Automobile Dealers Association, a dealer can't realize as much profit on warranty work as he would on the same work done out of warranty. The factory, said the NADA, allows a 25 percent markup on parts used in warranty repairs, while parts sold to nonwarranty customers are marked up 33 to 40 percent. Then there's the added paperwork in filing a warranty claim and the low factory payments to mechanics. It all explains the icy reception you often receive when you drive into a dealer with a clanking under the hood and a valid warranty in your pocket!

The flat-rate system also encourages outright dishonesty. Most mechanics are paid on a piece-work basis, usually receiving a 40-percent commission at dealerships on all work performed and as much as 60 percent in some independent garages and service stations. This system encourages slipshod workmanship and penalizes the meticulous mechanic who works carefully. I have a friend, a highly skilled and conscientious mechanic, who was fired from a large dealership simply because he was spending too much time on the cars to which he was assigned. He went to work a few days later in a large independent garage that deservedly enjoys an excellent reputation and was given a raise within two weeks as an endorsement of his good work. Maybe that is an isolated example, but I find it to be quite typical. The turnover among mechanics working in dealerships is outrageously high simply because the better tradesmen move on to greener pastures where they are paid according to their skills.

Many times it is still easier for a mechanic simply to fix a part, wipe it clean (or paint it), and then charge the customer for a new part, while picking up a commission on the cost of the new part at the same time. With such opportunities as these available to the unscrupulous, it's surprising that there are still so many honest mechanics around. But the alarming fact is that a good many are not. And what's worse, it is difficult to recognize the difference until you've already been victimized.

Even more disturbing is the fact that there are so few standards governing the qualifications of auto mechanics in this country that a customer has no way of knowing (except by word-of-mouth recommendation) whether he is leaving his car in the hands of a skilled tradesman or a blundering incompetent. Nearly every trade and profession in the world that provides some sort of service for the public is governed by some union or other organization that establishes standards of skill or ethics. A journeyman's card will quickly tell you how much training and experience a carpenter or a plumber has, but there are no such standards in most states governing the skills of the man who may fix the brakes on your car—even though your life could well depend on those skills. And, as incredible as it seems, most efforts by consumer groups, a few legislators, and even some auto-repair trade organizations have either been beaten down or resulted in watered-down versions that still come a long way from establishing reliable standards. But we will cover this unfortunate situation in more detail in the following chapter.

While incompetence might be difficult to control, outright dishonesty shouldn't be. But the attitude of many law-enforcement agencies around the country appears to be shockingly apathetic. Increased investigation of car-repair fraud "is not a priority item of the San Diego Police Department," admits Ray Hoobler, that city's Chief of Police.

"Some judges think it's un-American to prosecute a businessman," adds one big-city consumer attorney.

These are capsule comments on law enforcement in the field of automotive repair fraud. And, unfortunately, they are typical. Everyone, from policemen to attorneys to judges, agrees the problem is a serious one. But where they disagree is on how to cope with the problem. As costs go up and warranty periods go down, everyone seems to have someone else to blame. Consumer groups blame manufacturers, customers blame repair shops, and repairmen blame inflation.

At the same time, all agree that only a minority of dealers and repairmen are involved in actual fraud, that most are ethical in their dealings with customers. Nevertheless, fraud continues, and the number of complaints each year is growing. In 1972 there were 1483 complaints concerning automobile repairs, towing, and sales made to the New York City Consumer Affairs Department. One year later the number of complaints had jumped to 2031. And in just the first six months of 1974, the total had already reached 1146. Nor does the problem appear to be the exclusive property of big cities or heavily populated areas. Throughout Massachusetts, auto complaints increased more than seven-fold between 1967 and 1971, and other states show similar increases. Robert C. Alexander, head of California's comprehensive Auto Repair Bureau, said he found 5000 complaints awaiting him when he took office in 1971 when the bureau was formed. The following year—partly, it's true, because of the bureau's existence and ability to handle complaints—the number had skyrocketed to 44,000!

On a national level, the federal Office of Consumer Affairs in Washington reports that consumer complaints have been rising in recent years. Mostly, it says, over incompetence rather than outright fraud. A federal study shows that shoddy or unperformed work headed the list, followed by complaints involving warranty, defective parts, overcharges, slow delivery, and fraudulent practices.

New York's Michael Kraft blames the problems in that state and California partly on geography. In these areas, he explains, a huge concentrated population means more drivers, more cars, and, as a result, less interest in dealers and repairmen in repeat business. The story seems the same across the nation, however. Especially in the larger metropolitan areas. The *Minneapolis Star*, a newspaper noted for its consumer affairs reporting, conducted a lengthy and thorough investigation of auto-repair shops in 1974 and came up with some startling, if not encouraging, facts.

To assess the quality of auto repair in Minneapolis and its suburbs, the newspaper conducted a 12-week survey of 26 car-repair facilities. Each was visited twice in one of the six cars used in the survey. Reporters made 52 visits with their cars and in 12 of those visits were sold repairs judged unnecessary by a technical consultant who maintained the cars and rigged them for the study. The work and charges were satisfactory in the other visits. Charges for the unnecessary work ranged from $3.50 for carburetor adjustment to $191.13 for work on a transmission.

Also important to note was the fact that the team did discover that good, inexpensive, and efficient service was widely available. Fifteen times, the team reported, the test cars were repaired for $1 or less. Only two of the 52 visits to repair shops resulted in no correction of the problem.

Cars for the investigation were provided by a leasing company owned by the newspaper and were used solely for the investigation during the time reporters were visiting repair facilities. The six cars used were a 1972 Ford Galaxie, a 1972 Chevrolet Caprice, a 1972 Plymouth Fury, a 1967 Pontiac Bonneville, a 1970 Buick Electra, and a

1966 Volkswagen Beetle. The cars were put in top working order before being used for the investigation, except for the rigged defects. The two reporters, Suzanne Hovik and Peter Vaughan, visited service stations, independent garages, and new-car dealerships. What they discovered was a generally high level of competency—but questionable ethics— among car repair shops in the area.

In one case, the team drove into a service station after the right front brake on the VW had been tightened to the point where turning the wheel was almost impossible. The mechanic at the gas station was told that the car pulled severely to the right each time the brakes were applied. The reporter explained that she wanted the brakes checked and the pull corrected. The defect had been rigged in less than five minutes with nothing more than a screwdriver by Dale Feste, an instructor of auto mechanics at a local high school.

Feste said that a reasonable cost for correcting the problem should run from $5 to $15. All that was needed, he said, was to adjust the brakes, undoing the screwdriver work he had just performed.

But the crew at the friendly service station had bigger plans for Ms. Hovik and her aging VW. She was told that the mechanics were very busy and that she would have to leave the car for them to examine later in the day. The reporter called back that afternoon but was told the mechanic had just started to look at the car. When she called back again about half an hour later, Ms. Hovik was informed that something was wrong with the wheel cylinders. They weren't releasing, she was told. The estimated cost of the repair would be around $22—and the car wouldn't be ready until the next morning.

The reporters called the next morning and were informed that the work had been completed. Not only had the wheel cylinders been worked on, new front-brake shoes had been installed too. When Ms. Hovik picked up the car later in the day, she was handed a bill for $22.50. There was no breakdown on the bill for the new brake shoes, cylinder kit, the work on the cylinders, or the labor necessary to replace the brake shoes.

The reporters asked for and received the old brake shoes which, according to the repairman at the station, were well worn, "close to the rivets." But Feste had installed the brake shoes new only two weeks earlier. They had been driven less than 200 miles when the car was taken into the service station.

The wheel cylinders, Feste said, also were new and did not need repairing. There was no mention on the bill of the work that was necessary to adjust the brakes correctly. All the charges were for work considered by Feste to have been totally unnecessary. The brakes were satisfactorily adjusted, however.

Bob Palmer, owner of the Mobil station where this happened, defended his selling practices. "When you are in business, you try to sell, right?" Palmer was quoted by the *Star* as saying when reporters confronted him. He added that the consumer was always told when new parts were going to be put in and could always refuse them if they were not needed. Palmer said he didn't believe there was anything wrong with selling unnecessary parts.

"It's just like when someone sells me something I don't need, I take it. That's beside the point. I take it of my own free will," he said.

Two weeks earlier the team had visited the same service station in the same car, but this time it was rigged with a loose spark plug wire which reduced its already modest power source by 25 percent. At three other repair facilities the problem was corrected in minutes without charge.

But not at Palmer's.

Here's the account by reporters of what happened.

"We brought the VW into Palmer's at about 10 A.M. on March 27 [1974]. We described the problem (it seems to have lost its zip) and were told to call back a couple of hours later. We did and were told that the car was being road tested. We were also informed that the problem was in the carburetor.

"It didn't have enough poop, it didn't have enough gas going into it, and dirt had also gotten into the carburetor, we were told.

"The spark plugs and points, the man at Palmer's told us, 'looked pretty good.' (Feste had given the VW a complete tune-up only days before.)

"When we picked up the car later, we were billed $22.50 for checking the plugs and points, removing and cleaning the carburetor, and checking the timing and compression. There was no mention of the disconnected plug wire. If that had been found initially, our mechanic said, there would have been no reason for further diagnosis because the car would have run fine. When we picked up the car, the wire had been reattached. He (Feste) also concluded that 'the defect should have been found initially. It was simple to spot.' "

But here's the real kicker. And it happens so often.

After leaving Palmer's, the reporters noticed that the VW ran roughly at speeds approaching 50 miles per hour. When the car was checked out later in the evening, Feste discovered that the distributor cap had not been replaced correctly and was loose on one side, causing the engine to misfire and run roughly at higher speeds.

Although outright fraud appeared to be the biggest malady in the auto-repair industry in and around Minneapolis, there was also an unnecessary amount of obvious incompetence. For example: The team drove their 1972 Ford Galaxie into a local Ford dealership with the linkage joining the accelerator pump and the carburetor disconnected. This caused the car to hesitate noticeably when the driver attempted to accelerate at moderate speed on the highway. By any standards, it was an easy repair to spot and make—easy for a competent mechanic. The repair could have been made simply by reconnecting the pump linkage with a small clip. Aside from this planted defect, the car's carburetor was diagnosed by the newspaper's mechanic to be in tip-top shape.

Five hours after the Ford was taken into the dealership the reporters emerged with the car and a bill for $35.60 for overhauling the carburetor. Feste had said the repair could be performed easily for $3 to $15—depending upon whether the mechanic spotted the trouble immediately or employed diagnostic equipment.

Incompetence or fraud? Perhaps a little of both in this case. When Feste reexamined the car later that day, he not only confirmed that no work had been needed on the carburetor, but he also found that two parts of the "repaired" carburetor were missing! It cost an additional $10 to replace them.

Not enough is being done in most states to combat outright fraud, let alone incompetence. And that's the main reason both continue to flourish. The deck is stacked.

"There are too many of them and not enough of us," says Sgt. Ken Carpenter of the Los Angeles Police Department, rated as the nation's number-one car-fraud buster. To the car owner who has been taken, either by a salesman or a mechanic, it all adds up to frustration. Too often with little or no satisfaction.

Carpenter and his three-man squad initiate more than 150 prosecutions a year. That's more, he says, than are brought by all other prosecuting agencies in the state put together. His conviction ratio is an astonishing 98 percent. Yet he doesn't feel the war is being won. Not with 15 million vehicles on the state's highways, with 10,000 repair shops, with 38,000 mechanics, and with only a handful of lawmen willing and able to tackle the problem.

The California Automotive Repair Act, an amendment to the state's Business and Professions Code, went into effect on March 4, 1972. One of its most important provisions states that mechanics must provide written estimates which they may not exceed without the customer's approval and that they may not charge the customer for any unauthorized work. Violations can cost $500 and six months in jail. Carpenter thinks the law is a good one—"It's given us more teeth"— but he doesn't believe it has succeeded in lessening the problem.

"Without enforcement," he says, "the law is *nothing*. The mere fact that there is a law doesn't scare anybody. Unless your police are willing to go after these people they are going to keep on doing what they've been doing all along."

The existence of Carpenter's squad and its three undercover cars rigged to expose phony repair estimates has been well publicized in Los Angeles. "Every mechanic in town knows about us," says Carpenter, "but we're getting just as many fraud complaints as we did three years ago, maybe more."

All the business practices outlawed by the Automotive Repair Act continue unabated, Carpenter says. "False estimates, no estimates at all, overcharging, unnecessary work, unauthorized work, all kinds of misrepresentation—it still goes on. I don't understand it. Maybe it's because there are thousands of them and only four of us, and they figure we'll never get around to them."

The very complaints that the Automotive Repair Act was aimed at keep cropping up, most of them against the same shops. The number of offenders is but a small fraction of the thousands of shops and garages throughout this mobile state, but the number of offenses is disproportionately higher. The shops which do give rise to complaints appear to do it on a regular basis. Business is thriving.

"Dishonesty will not be stopped until we make it unprofitable to be dishonest," says one prominent California attorney who specializes in consumer cases. "And we're a long way from doing that."

He blames the lack of consumer protection on law-enforcement agencies, on judges, and on men like himself—attorneys in private practice.

"The main problem is that consumer cases are not serious enough to get the law-enforcement agencies involved, they don't entail enough money to get the regular attorneys interested, they are regarded as nuisances by more than a few judges, and they are easily mishandled by an attorney who is not an expert in the field."

All this adds up to "not enough prosecutions, not enough convictions, and not enough punitive damages to have any real deterrent value." What has to happen, he said, is that consumer-fraud cases will have to be handled on a routine basis, just like any other crime, by both law-enforcement agencies and private lawyers.

In most cases of auto-repair fraud, prosecutors can go either the criminal or the civil route. If they go criminal, they can get jail terms plus probation plus a fine, usually no more than $500 in most states; if they go civil, they cannot get jail terms, but they can ask for heavy penalties. This can add up fast. In one auto-fraud case in Santa Barbara, California, a firm was convicted of 32 violations and ordered to pay a whopping $80,000! There seems little doubt that if more culprits in this game were prosecuted that severely, auto-repair fraud wouldn't seem quite so attractive or lucrative to unscrupulous members of the industry.

This prosecution was carried out under one of the more significant new consumer laws in California. Under this law, prosecutors are given the option of regarding almost any type of business fraud as a violation of the Civil Code's unfair-competition statutes. Thus a case which formerly had to be prosecuted as a criminal misdemeanor—with a maximum fine of $500—can now be handled as a civil case instead, with the possibility of thousands of dollars in fines.

Pointing to the "reluctance of judges and juries to place white-collar criminals in jail," California's Deputy Attorney General Al Shelden says the next best deterrent would be the heavy penalties now available under this latest business-fraud section.

"This section is a great tool which should be utilized at every opportunity," Shelden said. "While prosecution as a misdemeanor may only result in a suspended sentence and a simple fine, the same violation prosecuted civilly will expose the violator to large civil penalties and injunctive orders. The penalties can be large enough to be effective against even the largest corporations and chains."

The contention that many private lawyers lack expertise in the consumer-fraud field is supported by a good many legal experts around the country.

"I think too often lawyers have just used the classical approach—fraud or misrepresentation—without doing some research on the other remedies available now," says Earl J. Cantos, presiding judge of the Special Proceedings Department of the San Diego Municipal Court. Many times, Cantos adds, he has seen cases where "there were defenses available that weren't used, and where there were remedies available that weren't even thought of."

And prominent California attorney John Barrett bemoans the sluggishness of so many lawyers to keep up with the times.

"I don't think there's any question that there is always a considerable time lag between the date a law is enacted and the time a sufficient number of attorneys become familiar with it."

And so confusion reigns in the auto-repair business—with car owners across the country as the most frequent victims. The remaining chapters of this book, however, are designed to give you some valuable ammunition for self-defense.

Chapter 2

How Good Is Your Mechanic?

Incompetence is not illegal. Not in the car-repair business, it isn't. The mechanic who robs you on purpose can be prosecuted. The one who does it unwittingly can't.

To the motorist stuck with a bill for unnecessary or shoddy work, it might not matter whether he is the victim of dishonesty or incompetence—to the law, it does.

"There are no criminal statutes against not knowing your job," says Jim Lorenz, Deputy District Attorney for San Diego in charge of fraud. "There's simply nothing a public prosecutor can do unless it's a case of fraud."

Owning an automobile may be part of the American dream, but for many millions of motorists across the country keeping that car running is a recurring nightmare. Americans pay out roughly $30 billion a year to service and repair their more than 110 million cars. A Senate subcommittee, after a three-year investigation into the auto-repair industry, estimated $10 billion of this was wasted on shoddy, unneeded, and overpriced work. How much of that is simply based on incompetence is difficult, if not impossible, to estimate. I suspect the percentage is absurdly high.

Testimony at the Senate hearings of the Subcommittee on Antitrust and Monopoly from automobile company executives, insurance officials, mechanics, and corporate critics painted a picture of an industry infected with greed, price gouging, lack of regulation, incompetence, and monopolistic controls.

"It was clear that the consumer who got his car fixed right the first try may be just plain lucky," was the conclusion of Senator Philip A. Hart, the Michigan Democrat who chaired the Senate hearings.

Examples abound. Take the case of schoolteacher Robert C. Miller of El Cajon, California, who bought a new camper one summer and enjoyed it until the first rains. It was then that he discovered a leak. Miller returned the camper to the dealer for repair. When the next rain came, it still leaked. Back to the shop.

Two days later, Miller was assured the problem had been corrected. But two months after that, Miller ran his camper through a car wash. It leaked. Back to the shop.

This time, after having it "fixed," Miller tested it with a garden hose. It still leaked. Back to the shop. Again, it was fixed.

A few months later—it was now July of the following year—he had his camper washed again. It leaked. In the same place, we should add. Back to the shop.

Two weeks later, Miller picked up the camper once again. He took it home and turned on the hose. You guessed it.

Miller was exasperated. He fired off a letter to the District Attorney. But he never did get any satisfaction. When he finally sold his camper a few months later, it was still leaking. This, says Lorenz, is a perfect example of a buyer's being victimized by incompetence and the law's being helpless.

"There is no way we could have shown intent to defraud," the attorney said. Other public prosecutors and investigators across the country echo the same sentiment and disillusionment with the status quo. But any remedy seems far off in most states.

Another case of frustration with the repair industry was that of Mr. and Mrs. Therman B. Oldhan, also of southern California. The Oldhans were slightly annoyed by the small "clattering or knocking" noise their five-year-old luxury car made when cold. They took it to a dealer. The next day the service manager called and said the car needed a complete engine overhaul. Oldhan approved the work. It cost him $927.85.

The morning after picking up his car, he started it. There was a familiar sound. Clattering or knocking. He took the car back. Some work was done, but the noise continued. After several more trips to the shop, Oldhan was told that the noise was something he would just have to live with. It couldn't be fixed.

"We finally tried to trade it in just to get out from under it," Oldhan recalls. He tried the dealer who had done the work. The dealer offered him only $800 ($500 below the value listed in the Kelley Blue Book), Oldhan says. "They said the car had a knocking noise and they'd have to fix it before they could sell it again."

The California Bureau of Automotive Repairs believes that incompetence is, in terms of dollars lost, a far greater problem than outright fraud. State Senator Anthony C. Beilenson, an outspoken Democrat from Los Angeles, calls it the number-one consumer problem in the nation. As it stands now, says Beilenson, "state law permits incompetent mechanics to represent themselves to the public as experts. That in itself is certainly a sham."

It's the same story, with only minor variations, throughout the entire country. Anyone may be a mechanic—just by buying some tools, renting garage space, and hanging up a sign that says so. More than 60 trades and professions in this country, from embalmers to barbers, require licensing and some apprenticeship training. But not car mechanics.

There is one thing, however, to keep in mind. Once the work is done you may have to pay the bill anyway, regardless of how satisfactory the job. It's too late for second thoughts. You'll never know whether you have invested in safety or in the auto mechanics' "charity fund." That piece of paper you sign when you leave your car for repairs carries considerable clout. It's not simply a "work order," as it's so often called. A mechanic's lien actually entitles the garage to keep your car until you pay the bill, and the garage doesn't even have to prove that the charges are legitimate. If you refuse to pay, the garage can sell your car for the cost of repairs and keep the money.

One of the most substantial cases on file relating to this predicament is that of college student Anthony R. Pedulla, who took his ailing car to a shop and received a verbal estimate of "around $50 or, at most, $100." Three days later a mechanic called and informed Pedulla that the problem was a little more complicated than first thought and the cost would be "well over $100."

Pedulla told the mechanic that as a college student he could not afford that much and asked him not to start work on the car; he'd pick it up the next day. When he arrived, Pedulla found his "engine scattered all over the floor." The mechanic said he had taken it upon himself to start repairs because he could do the job for "only $125."

Pedulla refused to accept this. In that case, the mechanic told him, he could have his car back "as is," with the engine dismantled, for a $50 labor charge. If Pedulla refused to pay, the mechanic said, he would not release the car and would charge storage fees at the rate of $2 per day. Pedulla wound up paying the $125.

District attorney and consumer group files around the country are filled with such incidents. In one case, a motorist took his car in for an advertised $119.50 ring and valve job and was charged $380 for a complete engine overhaul which he had not authorized. Or needed, in his opinion.

In another incident, a car owner was quoted $328 for a rebuilding job, but was billed $752, including "storage fees." It was those storage fees that really incensed him. He knew his car wasn't stored. It was parked on the street. And he had six parking tickets to prove it.

With machinery as complex as an engine or a transmission, it is often impossible for a mechanic to estimate accurately the full extent of repairs necessary without actually looking at the innards. Therefore, there is usually ample justification for revising an estimate for engine or transmission repair after an internal inspection.

Most parts of an automobile, however, can be checked externally with accuracy, and there should be no excuse for wrong estimates and bad repairs. If they do occur, it's usually a case of incompetency or fraud.

One factor working in favor of the repair shop, and against the car owner, is the "point of no return," that moment when the owner decides he has put so much money into repair already that he can't afford to unload the car and so digs himself a deeper hole.

"I don't know of any other business where so much good money is thrown after bad," says one consumer expert. "The trouble is, the car owner usually doesn't have much choice. If he can establish evidence of fraud, he can make a criminal complaint, but in most cases it's a matter of pure incompetency. A man can go from one incompetent mechanic to another and go deeper and deeper in debt, without any legal recourse."

Often the total repair bill far exceeds the value of the car. Many reputable repair shops will advise their customers on the economics of major repairs on older cars. But the greedy, dishonest, and incompetent one won't.

Mrs. Wanda Sutton took her car in to have a gear-shifting problem and noisy differential corrected. The shop talked her into a rebuilt engine, new carburetor, clutch plate, bearings, and other parts. The bill came to $651. The car was an 11-year-old Studebaker with a resale value so low that it wasn't even listed in the Kelley Blue Book.

The mechanic's lien is in force today in most states. But some consumer groups and activist lawyers are now beginning to challenge it—successfully in some cases.

In the early days of the automobile, mechanics felt they needed some sort of legal protection from car owners who wouldn't pay their bills.

The mechanics discovered that repairing a car was like healing the sick—you can't take back what you have done, even if you don't get paid for it. As early as 1914, the Arkansas Court of Appeal upheld the mechanic's lien, extending it to include labor charges as well as the cost of materials. As the law reads today, the repairman need only make a claim for a certain amount of money. It's a law that entitles the mechanic to keep the car as security for payment of the repair bill. Whether the repairs were proper, justified, authorized, or even legal is a side issue, one which has to be resolved in court. If the owner refuses to pay, no matter how valid his reason, the mechanic has the right to sell the car to satisfy his claim.

A repairman can start lien-sale proceedings within a few days (ten days in most states) of failure to pay. He can give notice of the sale in any newspaper of "general circulation," which means he doesn't have to use a paper with a large circulation. Any small suburban sheet will fill the bill. He'll sell the car to the highest bidder, and if the price isn't enough to cover the debt plus costs of the sale, he can still take the customer to court for the balance of the debt.

But attorney Ken Roye of the San Diego Legal Aid Society is among the growing number of lawyers throughout the country who don't think much of the way these sales are often conducted.

"Usually there is only a very small number of prospective buyers, often just friends and relatives of the mechanic," Roye explained. "The price obtained is often far below the market value of the car."

In many cases the car is purchased by an employee of the shop conducting the sale. Despite its original intent, the mechanic's lien has too often turned into a tool for unscrupulous mechanics to actually extort money from unwary customers. It's for this reason that many consumer lawyers are challenging its validity. Roye believes the law violates the constitutional right of due process. "No property may be seized without an equitable hearing for both parties," he says.

The law has been challenged successfully in lower courts on these grounds. In Texas the right to sell a person's property, even with a lien on it, without a court hearing was ruled unconstitutional, and on August 21, 1973, Municipal Judge Stuart C. Wilson of the San Diego County Judicial District Court ruled the underlying statute unconstitutional. He said it violated the constitutional guarantees against deprivation of property without due process. Ultimately, Roye thinks, the issue will be settled by the Supreme Court of the United States.

There is, of course, one sure-fire defense. You're safe from a mechanic's lien if you don't own your car outright. If you're still making payments, no one can sell your car because the new owner must be provided with a certificate of title. You could take it upon yourself to fight the system by writing a check and then stopping payment or simply by getting in the car and driving off—assuming, of course, that the mechanic won't try to detain you physically. Either way, there are some legal implications that could put you on the wrong end of the legal stick.

Technically, the mechanic could charge you with larceny. In practice, however, this isn't likely to happen. Even if it does, you would still have the advantage. Pressing criminal charges wouldn't get the mechanic his money. To do that he would have to file a claim in civil court and then prove that the repairs and charges are legitimate. Considering the time and expense involved in this kind of legal battle, the mechanic is put at a disadvantage. Should he decide to press criminal charges, you would have a sound defense since there is a legitimate dispute over the legality of the charges.

Legal experts advise making sure you have sufficient funds in your bank account to cover the check before stopping payment or you could be accused of writing a bad check. Technically, you may be guilty of ordering work under false pretenses, but in reality you are forcing the mechanic to explain the charges or otherwise justify his work. This is a legitimate beef. According to legal counselors, having a bona fide dispute is an effective defense against false-pretense charges.

The best idea, of course, is to avoid getting yourself in situations like this in the first place. There are several ways of protecting yourself against unauthorized repairs and avoiding the experience of returning to pick up your car and finding the bill twice as much as you expected. To begin with, take a few precautions when signing the repair order by making a few simple modifications. Always ask for an estimate and have the mechanic or whoever is writing up the repair order look up all charges in the flat-rate manual, which about 90 percent of all garages and dealer service departments use. If your garage doesn't use the flat-rate scale, ask what the hourly labor charge is. Be sure all the amounts, for both labor and material, are filled in before you sign. Cross out any blank lines on the order after all the work to be done and all the parts to be used are listed. Then be sure to initial all repairs and all parts to be used. Before signing, add "for repairs initialed hereunder" to the paragraph that appears just above where you sign your name.

This paragraph usually includes acknowledgment of a mechanic's lien and reads roughly as follows: "I hereby authorize the repair work hereinafter set forth to be done along with the necessary material, and hereby grant you and/or your employees permission to operate the car or truck herein described on streets, highways, or elsewhere for the purpose of testing and/or inspection. An express mechanic's lien is hereby acknowledged on above car or truck to secure the amount of repairs thereto."

You should delete the word "thereto" and add "initialed hereunder."

While this prevents the mechanic from sticking you with unnecessary work, it also has some drawbacks. If he discovers other needed repairs he will have to contact you by phone before going ahead with them. But he may also be reluctant to make any additional repairs without written authorization, since he lacks a lien on such work even if he has your verbal approval. But this is obviously a small risk compared with what you're facing otherwise. Leaving all those blank spaces on a work order is like handing someone a signed blank check.

Roy Kramer, a Chicago salesman, learned that the hard way. He took his aging station wagon into one of those large chain garages for two new tires. The service manager also urged Kramer to have his wheels balanced and suggested possibly having the mechanic check the car to see if it needed a front-end alignment. Kramer agreed. The service manager then made out a work order for two tires and added wheel balancing and alignment to the list. The estimate came to $67.82. Kramer signed it and left for work with a colleague. But when he returned that evening to pick up his car he was handed a bill for $278.03 for two tires, shocks, tie rod bushings, idler arm, valve stems, and wheel packing.

Whether the work was actually necessary, of course, is debatable. Kramer felt he had a case, but he made one mistake. He paid the bill before consulting an attorney. It cost him another $40 to hear a lawyer tell him a few days later that it didn't look like he had more than a snowball's chance in hell of getting any kind of satisfaction since he had, in essence, given the garage carte blanche by signing an incomplete work order. Kramer filed a complaint with the District Attorney's office, which was added to an already bulging file of similar complaints against the same garage.

Sometimes even shopping around first to get several estimates can be confusing. Karl Doyle of Houston was having trouble starting his car every morning. Wary of mechanics, Doyle took his car to four garages to get estimates of what was wrong and what it would cost. Two mechanics told him frankly that they didn't know and would have to check it out before even giving an estimate. One garageman said he was sure the car needed new points, while another insisted that only a complete tuneup would correct the trouble. Each approach sounded plausible. Who was right?

"Probably the man with the lowest estimate," says attorney Jim Lorenz. "Although, as a lawyer, I could not advise anyone against repairs which half a dozen mechanics might swear are valid or essential to safety."

The two mechanics who admitted they didn't know could have been honest, and probably were. Troubleshooting isn't always easy, and it is rarely an exact science except in the case of legitimate diagnostic centers which utilize elaborate and sophisticated equipment. But honest or not, they could also be blundering incompetents learning by trial and error at your expense. On the other hand, the guy who recommended a major tuneup as the only sure cure might well have put Doyle's car in good running condition, but he might also have been trying to sell Doyle a lot of unnecessary goods. And the repairman who diagnosed the problem as worn-out points could have been either a top troubleshooter, simply guessing, or trying to lure a victim into his shop, hoping to make a bigger score later.

The trouble is, you can't always tell until it's too late. In this case, the two mechanics who admitted they didn't know were more than likely honest and accurate since a hard-starting car can be caused by any number or combination of things, including worn points, bad spark plugs or spark plug cables, a tired distributor or cracked distributor cap, an aging coil, or a reluctant carburetor needing adjustments or perhaps even a complete overhaul. The list doesn't necessarily end there, but that gives you some idea of the situation.

The best mechanic I have ever encountered, a gentleman named Nik, will never hazard a guess as to what is wrong with a customer's car or make even an educated guess at what it will cost to fix until he has personally examined the machine at length. Then he will tell you exactly what is wrong and how much it will cost—sometimes right down to the penny, including tax. On top of this, he always guarantees his work for 90 days. This is the way it should be, and would be throughout the country, if we only had stiffer controls and requirements on mechanics. This man is a complete professional, who served a lengthy apprenticeship in Europe and worked in Holland and Germany for several years as a journeyman before coming to the United States. The only hassle involved in having him work on your car is that it usually takes anywhere from two weeks to a month to get an appointment. This is sometimes an inconvenience, but it is a small one considering the alternatives. He never advertises. His customers take care of that.

Is he unique? In these United States, he is rare to be sure. Like a breath of fresh air in downtown Los Angeles. But in Europe and Canada, all mechanics must complete a rigorous training program, pass tough exams, and serve under a certified mechanic for from three to five years. No one is permitted to serve as an auto mechanic without earning either an A, a B, or a C certificate issued by the automobile trade governing body. This indicates his abilities and standards of skill to any potential employer or customer. During their training, European apprentices learn how to use lathes, grinders, drilling machines, and anything else that might help them be better mechanics. The result is a highly respected trade of skilled repairmen—in sharp contrast to the many blundering parts changers that dominate the industry here. It's not surprising that a European auto repairman can better diagnose the trouble, quote an accurate estimate, and smugly guarantee his work.

Most auto mechanics in this country do not know how to repair cars. They merely install new or rebuilt parts. Their training, for the most part, has been strictly by trial and error. Very often—too often, in fact—they learn by working and experimenting on your car and mine. Sometimes their experiments work out. Sometimes they don't. This kind of learning is euphemistically called "on-the-job-training." Under qualified supervision, that kind of training has a place in almost any trade or profession. But in most cases in this country there is little or no supervision from a certified expert, simply because we don't have many experts. Most of the really sharp mechanics in this country aren't repairing automobiles at the corner garage, they're more likely to be found tuning racing engines in the pits at Indianapolis or Daytona.

Another misleading term frequently used and abused in this country is "factory trained mechanic." In Europe this really means something. A mechanic who can boast of factory experience is talking about a genuine training program that ultimately produces outstanding specialists. These are advanced programs for seasoned repairmen, who then either go to work for a dealer or open their own shops and specialize in some such area of auto repair as transmission, suspension, brakes, or engine overhaul. When you leave your car in the hands of one of these experts you know it is going to get the best attention available. If your car can't be fixed or isn't worth spending money on, you will probably be told so.

A few years ago a friend wanted to put his aging foreign economy car in good shape in order to avoid laying out more money for a new or later model. He asked me to recommend a reliable mechanic. I sent him to Nik, who looked the car over carefully, drove it a couple of miles, and then turned to my friend and said soberly:

"I tell you what. You take car home, wash up nice, park in driveway, and put 'for sale' sign in window. No drive no more. Okay?"

Unaccustomed to that sort of candid advice from a humble wrench turner, my friend asked me what I thought he should do. I told him to follow the expert's advice exactly. But he elected instead to take the car into a gas station, where he was bilked out of nearly $200, for everything from an engine tune-up to shocks. And over the next six months my friend regretted his decision several times a week as the car continued to require inexpensive but aggravating repairs.

Later, I mentioned to Nik what had happened. He shook his head in dismay. "I try to tell him that car no good. Why he no listen?"

When I explained that it was primarily because so few of his colleagues in this country had the professional wisdom and esteem they enjoyed across the Atlantic, Nik seemed perplexed. At that time he had only been in this country for about two years. He isn't so naive anymore, but he is still just as honest.

A "factory trained mechanic" in this country is most probably someone who has attended a one-week (or perhaps two-day) seminar learning how to remove and replace some new part or gadget, or correct a defect which shouldn't have slipped into the design in the first place. Car manufacturers in this country neither train repairmen or mechanics, nor do they discourage their dealers from claiming they have factory trained personnel on duty. Of course, in a nation having no standards of performance for the people who are supposed to keep their fellow citizens on wheels, attending a two-day parts-changing seminar in Detroit no doubt seems like a big deal.

What an absurd situation in a country having more cars, more licensed drivers, and more miles of roads and super highways than any other country in the world! Of course, we also have more accidents, injuries, fatalities, and smog—all related in varying degrees to the poor quality of automobile service available. To compound the problem, no matter how unskilled mechanics are, their services are in short supply. According to professional estimates, this country is roughly 100,000 mechanics short of meeting current service needs, and the situation will inevitably grow worse over the next few years as the auto population continues to soar. There are roughly 130 cars in the United States today for every mechanic, compared with a ratio of about 80 to one only a decade ago.

Part of the problem is the low estimation we in this country have of tradespeople. In fact, young people are actively discouraged from entering the so-called blue-collar fields. Our high schools emphasize college preparatory courses at the expense of solid vocational training that would better prepare those who aren't interested in college to enter trade apprenticeship programs directly upon graduation from high school. A different view of education in this country might also serve to alleviate the dismal unemployment problem which is always concentrated among the unskilled members of our society.

But while we're rapping everyone from designers and corporate executives to dealer service departments, society itself, high schools, and the corner garage, it wouldn't be fair not to take a look at some positive changes taking place. Despite the aggravating and often expensive blunders built into so many of Detroit's products, U.S. auto makers are delivering a much better overall car to their customers now than they were ten or more years ago. As we mentioned earlier, engines, transmissions, and tires, if not abused or neglected, are much more reliable. And while there are few regulations governing the qualifications of auto mechanics, the industry itself is moving toward at least voluntary certification of auto repairmen. The first workable system, inspired primarily by the consumer revolt and its repercussions, was developed by the Independent Garage Owners of America in cooperation with the Automotive Service Industry Association and the National Congress of Petroleum Retailers. The qualification test they devised for auto mechanics covers 15 basic specialties ranging from frame repair to engine overhaul. By passing any of the specialties a mechanic can be certified by the National Automotive Technicians Certification Board. Any mechanic who passes eight of the first ten classifications is then rated by the NATCB as a Master Technician. These tests are far from easy and require a solid background and extensive knowledge.

Still another mechanic's qualification test is now available through the National Automobile Dealer's Association, which developed a comprehensive 12-hour examination with the help of the Educational Testing Service of Princeton, an organization better known for its College Board Exams. Passing this test qualifies an applicant as a Certified General Automobile Mechanic (GAM) through an organization called the National Institute for Automotive Service Excellence. Both the NATCB and GAM programs require proof that an applicant has worked as a mechanic for at least two years.

If these certification programs are successful, at least within their limited capacity, it will be possible to know just how qualified a mechanic is before he begins turning a wrench on your car. None of these efforts, of course, will necessarily rid the industry of its dishonest members, but it should at least weed out most of the criminally inept. And that's a good beginning.

But that leaves us with the big question. Will all mechanics take the test or tests without being required by law to do so? Probably not. And *that's* the major weakness inherent in such a voluntary system. So, until state or federal laws require licensing and certification of all auto mechanics (and please don't hold your breath!), you are going to have to watch out for yourself to avoid being gypped or victimized by both fraud and incompetence.

Chapter 3
Watch for These Common Frauds

Nobody knows exactly how much fraudulent auto repairs cost motorists each year in this country, but investigations by law-enforcement agencies in California and Arizona place the amount at millions of dollars from service station frauds alone. Following a 1972 investigation in California, officials estimated that consumers were being bilked out of more than $2 million a year just along Interstate 15, that much-traveled desert road between Los Angeles and Las Vegas.

I don't doubt it. A couple of years before that investigation I was automotive writer for a southern California daily newspaper and made the trip to see for myself after our office had received numerous complaints from readers. The car I drove was in good running condition (excellent by most standards), but at nearly every stop attendants tried to sell me just about everything—from carburetor air filters to windshield-wiper blades. None of them, to my knowledge, actually tried to sabotage the car, but that may have been primarily because I was watching them every moment. And that kept me busy, because at some stops two and even three attendants swarmed over the car.

Other common trouble spots, according to investigators, have been Route 66 in Arizona and Route 95 in Florida. Traveling motorists, easily identified by out-of-state plates, bug-splattered windshields, and loads of luggage are favorite prey. Away from home and anxious to continue their journey, travelers are less likely to question the need for repairs or replacements—regardless of cost. Women traveling alone or driving at night are also popular targets of auto-repair fraud artists. In each case, the fear of being stranded in a strange or isolated place serves as leverage for the shyster to talk his potential victims into unnecessary repair.

Following are some of the more common frauds you are likely to encounter, both at home and on the road, accompanied by tips on how to avoid them.

Tire Tricks

Of all the fraud gimmicks used by service station operators, tire tricks are about the easiest to pull off and among the most lucrative. The retail markup on tires is high, and changing rubber is one of the easiest jobs a mechanic is likely to encounter. Investigators in California, using undercover cars and mechanics, discovered a widespread tire-selling game that was bilking motorists out of thousands of dollars a month in and around the Los Angeles area alone.

Not surprisingly, the most common victims were vacationers from out of state who were eager to see all the attractions, such as Disneyland and the San Diego Zoo, and couldn't afford any delays in their already crowded schedules. The con game, with slight variations, usually goes like this.

The attendant voluntarily checks the air in your tires. As he does so, he lets out a few pounds instead of adding some. The next step is to notify you that such and such a tire (it will almost always be on the side away from the driver) is low and that, since it might have a leak, he'd like to check it again before you pull out. If you're like about 99 out of 100 motorists you will fall for the trick and be pleased that this alert young man is taking such an interest in you.

Of course, when he "checks the tire again" he finds that "it's still leaking" and asks you to take a look for yourself. He will probably tell you next that the tire apparently has a hole in it and that he can take it off and check it out for you, possibly even patch it. Since you are traveling and don't want to drive without a spare, you give him the go-ahead. In many cases the attendant may even recommend that you go across the street and have a cup of coffee at the local diner (probably owned and operated by his brother-in-law). This, to be sure, is a friendly gesture designed to get you out of the way so he will be more free to do his "work." But some slick con artists will be able to puncture a tire literally under your nose without being detected. Most of them use a screwdriver or a dart tip with a needle-sharp point. Some seasoned weasels even use a special ring called a "slasher" for puncturing tires.

Puncturing the tire guarantees the attendant that you will be convinced it's leaking. He will then submerge it in water and when it bubbles up, will nod knowingly and sympathetically. Too bad, too bad. But, alas, these things happen. Nails and glass on the road, you know.

But punctures can be patched quite easily, quickly, and cheaply. And there's little or no profit in patching tires. So, the ripoff artist must convince you that this tire isn't worth patching, or should not be patched for safety reasons. That's one of their favorite terms. It scares people.

"That always gits 'em," one former tire salesman confided a few years ago. "Tell a guy his family is riding on dangerous rubber and he about comes unglued!"

To prove the tire is too worn to patch, the attendant will turn it inside out and stretch the seams so they look worn and thin or split. He may, depending on his imagination, experience, and dramatic talents, utter a few exclamatory remarks like "Whew, look at that" or "Man, are you ever lucky you stopped in!" just to make sure you realize the urgency of the situation.

Most travelers won't go back out on the road without a spare in the trunk, so this routine almost always results in at least one tire sale. But if some customer is skeptical or reluctant to invest in a tire at the moment, the crooked attendant usually serves up his ace in the hole: offering helpfully to install the spare. He then uses a modified version of the first trick, so that you either have to drive out on three wheels or buy a new tire (and more than likely two, since they will conveniently be "on sale" this week).

You buy, naturally. Testimony from the trial of one such gypster in Los Angeles showed $8000 to $10,000 a month in tire sales from just such techniques. As an added incentive to such larceny, the punctured tires are usually patched later and then sold to other customers as good-quality used-tire bargains.

This kind of chicanery is most often discovered in what law officers and members of the auto industry refer to as "gypsy" service stations—those establishments along lonely stretches of deserted highway that usually sport signs saying things like "Last Chance for Gas," etc. Tires, batteries, and shock absorbers are the items most frequently sold by these operators. Their specialty is hustling.

You may find these operators anywhere, however. Not just along some lonesome desert highway. Complaints are pouring in almost daily to legal agencies in California, Arizona, New York, Florida, and Massachusetts. They seem to grow in number every year, despite mounting efforts by many law-enforcement agencies and consumer groups to stop such racketeering.

Nor are the crooks in this case maverick operators. According to the White House Office of Consumer Affairs, "the vast majority of complaints received about fraudulent service station practices involved the dealerships of major oil companies."

When queried about the situation, the usual response from these financial giants is, "Sorry, there is nothing we can do about our independent dealers." There are indications, however, that some oil companies are taking steps to keep closer tabs on their dealers through consumer-protection clauses in some of their service station leases. But this rarely amounts to more than keeping score on consumer complaints and following up only when one station operator appears to be attracting more than his share.

Perhaps the surest and simplest way to avoid the tire tricks is always to get out of your car when you stop at a gas station, unless it's one you patronize regularly. Watch what the attendant does. If you sit complacently inside your car and nod passively when the attendant asks, "Check under the hood?," you are inviting trouble. I asked my informant, the former tire hustler, how many people took the trouble to get out and observe his work. "Not one in fifty," he replied without hesitating. "If they did, I'd be hurtin'."

Checking Under the Hood

Almost before you can say "Fill 'er up," some slick attendants known in the trade as "tool men" can size you up as an easy mark and sabotage your car in a con game called "skinning the dude." In addition to slashing tires, radiator hoses, and fan belts, they are skilled at tricks designed to send unsuspecting motorists into near panic.

"Short-sticking" is one of the most common and easiest ploys. The attendant simply pushes the dipstick down part way and then reports your engine is low on oil. If you bite, he is then likely to take an empty can, turn it upside down, and insert the spout, pouring nothing more than air into your crankcase. It isn't a major ripoff, of course, but at the end of a successful day a real hustler can pick up enough change to treat the boys at the corner tavern to several rounds. Thanks to you.

The number of charades in this business is limited solely by the imagination and skill of the tool man. One of the most common, and yet lucrative, tricks is to pour an Alka Seltzer tablet or a few drops of dish detergent into the battery cells. The frothing and bubbling that results is almost certain to panic the majority of unwitting motorists, who are then ripe for convincing they need a replacement. Unless your battery is three years old or older and you have been having trouble with it, don't let one of these slick sleight-of-hand artists dupe you into buying a new one, or even getting the old one recharged. More often than not, battery problems are the result of corrosion built up on the terminals. You can fix this simply enough yourself by merely unscrewing the cables and clearing off any corrosive substance with a knife, screwdriver, or even fingernail file. Be sure to do each one separately to insure against mixing up the cables when you reconnect them. If you do buy a new battery, insist on keeping the old one so you can have it checked later to see if it was tampered with.

Still another under-the-hood trick is pouring a little barbecue sauce or meat curative on your car's alternator or generator. This results in a lot of white smoke and very often an $80 or $90 repair bill for those who fall for the pitch warning them that the only solution is immediate replacement of the worn-out part. To make sure the victim is convinced, the mechanic will often disconnect or loosen a battery cable or an ignition wire and then ask the driver to start the car. When it won't, it makes his story all the more convincing.

The smoke looks convincing too, but one smell will tell you it isn't from any fire. If the attendant has loosened a battery cable or an ignition wire, you can still check to see if the trouble is really the generator or alternator simply by turning on the ignition key without cranking the engine. If that red light on the dash goes on, it means somebody is putting *you* on. Generators rarely, if ever, smoke. They gradually quit doing their job, which means the battery takes over. If the generator or alternator in your car does go out, you can usually tell because the red light will continue to burn when the engine is running. A car equipped with a gauge instead of an idiot light will indicate a continuing discharge.

The incentive for this kind of larceny is the 50 percent cut many attendants earn on all auto parts and equipment they sell. California officials found that some of the top hustlers in San Bernardino County (mostly along the desert roads) were making up to $4000 a month. Once again, the simplest and surest way to avoid most of these skin games is to climb out of your car at unfamiliar stations and watch what the attendant does. Even the most brazen hustler or tool man isn't likely to pull any of his tricks while you are looking over his shoulder, whether you actually know what you're looking at or not.

The Lure

Some large franchised specialty shops advertise bargains on tires, batteries, engine tune-ups, and shock absorbers primarily as a lure to get you into the clutches of their "service managers" or "representatives" who know how to work on your fears and general ignorance of the automobile you drive. Once they have your car on the rack to install new tires or shocks, the mechanic will "discover" worn brakes or bad ball joints. Hearing this is usually enough to throw a scare into most car owners, which is exactly what the hokum servicemen count on.

One of my friends took his car into a large tire dealer for installation of new rubber on the front only, since he couldn't afford new tires all around at the time. While his car was on the rack and he was reading a magazine and sipping courtesy coffee in the waiting room, the service manager came in and told him the shocks were shot. My friend, following the advice of what he considered an expert, okayed installation of new shocks. About three months later his wife took the same car in for two more new tires, and guess what? The service manager told her the shocks were shot and explained how serious and potentially dangerous the situation was. Fortunately, she decided to give her husband a call to see what he thought about spending the extra money. She never imagined his response. Neither did the service manager!

It's too easy to check shock absorbers yourself to let anyone con you into replacing them. Simply push down on the fender over each wheel. If the car springs back into its normal position and stays there, the shocks are okay. If it bounces a little, then you may be needing new ones. Sometimes a clever tool man will squirt oil on shocks and report that they are leaking fluid and should be replaced. Thank him courteously, ask him to wipe the shocks clean (or do it yourself), wait two or three days, and then check the shock or shocks involved to see if more fluid is leaking. Chances are they will still be as clean as when they were wiped off earlier. You can usually tell immediately, however, if the mechanic is telling the truth. The fluid or grease will almost always be dirty and gritty if the shocks are actually leaking. If it looks fairly clean and fresh—watch out! It was more than likely poured or squirted on only a few minutes before it was pointed out to you. Even factory shock absorbers (which are not usually top quality) can last 20,000 miles or more, if you drive moderately on smooth roads. So, if the ones on your car have traveled fewer miles they may still have plenty of life left in them.

Crooked auto repairmen also specialize in ball joints because it is so easy to convince people that the ones on their cars are worn out. It's an old game, but it's still effective. The mechanic will usually shake the wheel when he has the car up on a rack. The wheel, of course, will wobble some, and the owner will be informed that this indicates bad ball joints. Baloney! Most automobiles are built with a certain amount of play in the wheels to allow for clearance and relieve tension. Get another opinion—or two or three. This trick, in fact, grew to be so common that General Motors started using self-adjusting ball joints in its 1973 models. The wheels on these cars don't wobble, so that old sham won't work any more.

Anytime a so-called mechanic says he discovered that the brakes on your car need repairing while he was changing tires or performing some other work, it is wise to thank him for being so helpful and get a few other opinions before approving any work. Brake work is too important to ignore, but it also can be expensive—especially if it isn't necessary to begin with. Nor is brake work a good exercise for "on-the-job training." Take your car into two or three shops that specialize in brake work and ask the fellows to look things over. Throwing money away on unnecessary or incompetent engine or transmission work may prove maddening, but doing the same on your car's brakes can end tragically. The California Highway Patrol, after a lengthy investigation, determined that 29 percent of all fatal accidents involved cars that were mechanically defective and that in most cases these defects caused or contributed to the accident. The CHP found faulty brakes to be the number-one culprit.

Transmission Troubles

Experts agree that no component of your automobile is more sensitive or complicated than the transmission. Consequently, it is also the most expensive and difficult to repair. Not surprisingly then, this mechanism is a favorite of the gypster who wants to make a lot of money for little or no work.

The most common trick goes something like this. You drive into the transmission shop or general garage complaining of transmission trouble. Maybe the gears grind when you shift or, if it is an automatic transmission, perhaps it seems to be slipping or making funny noises. The mechanic may or may not take your car for a road test, which won't matter anyway because all he wants is to get his hands on your money. Whether he goes for a road test or not, this guy will always explain that he can't diagnose the trouble until he tears down the transmission and examines its innards. This job, he says, will take him at least a day. But don't worry; he will call you as soon as he locates the trouble. The diagnosis may vary, but the price will almost always be between $200 and $300.

By now you may have decided to shop around or just to let it go for awhile. In either case you will be told that it will cost at least $75 to get the transmission put back together before you can even drive the car. You now have the choice of paying $75 for nothing or taking your chances on this guy's integrity and skill and sticking with him until the job is done. He, naturally, is counting on the latter. According to the U.S. Attorney's office in Washington, D.C., most motorists decide to go ahead and have the repairs made on the spot.

In this case, you have no doubt been taken. Automotive engineers estimate that 80 percent of all transmission repairs can be made without taking the unit apart.

Another frequent trick is for a mechanic to show you some metal shavings he has found in your car's automatic transmission. He says this indicates that the gears are worn out and need replacing. The truth is, the meshing of gears in most transmissions always produces a certain amount of metal filings. Sometimes the racket is even more subtle. The mechanic adjusts the rings and bands in the transmission and bills you $250 or more for an overhaul job. Or he may replace the vacuum modulator, a job that should cost between $25 and $40, and charges you $300 or more for rebuilding the unit.

As a rule, avoid transmission shops that advertise big in newspapers and on television and radio. These outfits are too often more interested in selling you a rebuilt gearbox than making minor repairs. Good transmission specialists rarely advertise much beyond a blurb in the Yellow Pages. They don't have to. Unless a particular shop or mechanic has been highly recommended by a knowledgeable friend, get at least two, and preferably three, estimates *in writing* of the trouble and the cost before authorizing anyone to begin repairs.

The Paint Bath

Many repair shops have the habit of painting such rebuilt parts as starter motors, fuel pumps, etc. This policy is basically innocent, but it opens the door to dishonest mechanics. What happens is this. A mechanic may replace the diaphragm in the fuel pump, spray a coat of paint on the larger mechanism, and bill you for a new or rebuilt part that may cost you ten times what the work was actually worth. Quite often the stakes are even higher if the mechanic is working on something like the transmission where he can make a $20 adjustment, use a can of paint, and bill you $200.

The best defense against this ripoff is twofold—either mark the various parts of your car that might be replaced or else ask to see the old parts. Better still, do both. If you can't find that dot or X you painted or etched on, better start hunting for an attorney.

Highway Robbery

Most dishonest mechanics wait patiently for their victims to come to them, but there is a breed of crook in this business who goes out after his prey. He's usually riding in a tow truck and looks like an angel of mercy to the stranded and unsuspecting motorist.

To be sure, most tow truck drivers are honest. But there are a few too many who aren't. These vultures are usually in cahoots with some garage down the road. Often their modus operandi is to listen to the police radio for accidents or to prowl the highways in search of stranded motorists. But before these rascals will tow you anywhere they ask you to sign a contract giving the tow truck operator exclusive rights to repair your car. *Don't sign.* The mechanic's lien and the salvage value of the car is more than enough to cover the cost of both the tow and the repair. Ask any tow truck driver who mysteriously happens along if he works for a garage. If he says yes, ask him to take your car to another place. Should he refuse, you will know he's working a racket. You will be better off waiting for a highway patrol officer or walking than doing business with this operator.

Keeping a list of known reliable towing services in your area is one way of avoiding such a predicament. Like most auto accidents, breakdowns usually happen within 25 miles of home, so you will be pretty well protected this way. If you want a more sure protection or are planning a trip of some distance, join the American Automobile Association's road-service program. You do not have to buy your auto insurance from AAA to qualify for the group's road service, and AAA polices the garages it contracts with, so the chances of just being towed instead of taken are in your favor.

Model Year Updating

So you bought a brand new little import this year. Straight from the showroom into your driveway. Your sales contract says it's new. Your registration says it's new. You paid for a new car. Does all this make it a new car?

Not necessarily. It's possible that only a few weeks before you bought it, your brand new car was sitting in the dealer's showroom being advertised as brand new, but listed as one year earlier than when you happened along. At the end of the model year, the car was still unsold. So the dealer simply updated it. He changed the year.

It happens. Not with domestic passenger cars which have new body styles nearly every year. But it happens with imports, and it happens with domestic trucks, campers, motor homes, and other recreational vehicles. A vehicle becomes a '74 or a '75 or a '76 because the manufacturer and dealer decide that this is what it should be. When the calendar says it's time for a new model, the buyer gets a new model. It's then sold as a current model. In terms of mileage and condition it is, indeed, new. But can the same car which was displayed with a 1975 sign on the windshield last year be sold as a '76 this year?

Yes, it can. A district attorney's investigator in one major city says the manager of a large dealership told him some time ago that this practice was "accepted by all dealers." He may have been overstating his case. Some dealers have close-out sales on last year's models well into the current year. But another dealer told the same investigator: "If we have a car left over, and we normally do, we'll change it and notify the state."

The California Department of Motor Vehicles says it does, in fact, receive "occasional" notification of model-year updating. However, the DMV does not require such notification. It is up to the dealer and the manufacturer. The DMV does not consider updating illegal. Some disagree.

"It's tantamount to fraud," says Bob Nida, attorney for the Automobile Club of Southern California. "When a man pays the new-car price and then finds out at trade-in time that his vehicle is actually a year older and its value less, then he has been taken advantage of."

Without the protection of legislation, the buyer of an updated car is pretty much on his own. As long as there is no law which defines the practice of updating as illegal, the car buyer may find that his only recourse is to hire a lawyer and sue for damages. And that may cost him more than he stands to gain. Which is usually the case.

"If he is awarded the difference in value between the two model years," says Nida, "it will probably cost him all of that in attorney's fees."

Sometimes the threat of legal action may be sufficient, however. A school teacher discovered a few weeks after buying his new import that it was really a year older. When he threatened to sue, the dealer agreed to reduce the price. This buyer was fortunate that he discovered the discrepancy quickly. Usually a driver does not find out his car is an updated version until he tries to sell it and the prospective buyer is knowledgeable enough to spot the difference. By that time, the one-year statute of limitations on misdemeanors has probably obviated criminal prosecution.

That leaves the buyer with only the alternative of civil action. But you had better be prepared to undertake that yourself, and at your own expense. The agencies which enforce the law of the land, the offices of the U.S. Attorney, the state attorneys general, the district attorneys, and city attorneys are all hesitant to take civil action.

"We'd rather not handle them," says Janet Kintner, a former Legal Aid Society firebrand who now works in the San Diego City Attorney's consumer fraud unit. "Civil cases involve a lot more time and a lot more work. Because of staff and time limitations we can do more criminal cases in the same amount of time."

The phrase used by the public prosecutor is "We, the People," and that's exactly what he means. Unless there is a significant number of victims or a considerable number of violations, chances are that no civil action will be forthcoming. So the victim turns to the local department of motor vehicles for help. One example is the case of a college instructor who bought a 1972 vehicle at a '72 price and took it on a cross-country trip. At the first stop for servicing, a mechanic told him he was driving a '71, not a '72. At the next stop, the man asked another mechanic. Same answer. At still a third stop he heard the same thing.

Convinced he had been cheated, the man returned to the dealer and asked for a new vehicle. He was turned down. He went to the DMV in his home state. No results. Then the Attorney General's office. Same thing. He turned next to a consumer fraud attorney, who took the case and tried the same approach. First the DMV.

"We got an answer saying that to their knowledge it was no violation of any existing law and they were powerless to intervene," says the attorney.

What about the Attorney General?

"That office declined to take action."

The next step was for the attorney to take the case directly to the manufacturer. After one year of correspondence, he got his answer. The manufacturer was quite satisfied with the status quo. Period. The end.

The practice of updating is considered a legal gray area. Most attorneys agree that the only way of turning it into black and white is through tough legislation at either the state or the federal level. Right now the gray appears to begin with the definition of "new car." What is a *new* car? Is it a car manufactured in the current year? Obviously not, since Detroit started building current models in the middle of last year. Is it a car manufactured for marketing this year? That would be difficult to reconcile with the philosophy of car makers like Daimler-Benz Corp., which pride themselves on introducing new models only when technological advances warrant it.

Then what *is* a new car?

Most state motor vehicle departments don't pretend to know or have an answer. Car registrations state clearly: "Year model is based on dealer and manufacturer representation."

Quinton Peters, Chief of Vehicle Registration in California, puts it succinctly: "We take their word for it."

But while the issue is nebulous legally, it is quite clear economically. The buyer of an updated car stands to lose money. The Kelley Blue Book, price guide for dealers and lending institutions, almost always—with rare exceptions—assigns a higher dollar value to a later-model car.

"Everything else being equal—model, mileage, condition—the new car will always be priced higher," says Robert S. Kelley, copublisher of the Blue Book. This is a policy set by the dealers themselves, he says. "We don't dictate to the market, we react to it."

The difference a year makes can range from less than $100 to well over $1000, depending on original purchase price and age of the car. How can we buyers protect ourselves? How do we tell the difference?

Sometimes there is no difference. A certain model may remain completely unchanged from one year to the next. This is especially true of imported cars. But even domestic models sometimes undergo only minimal changes. For example, the only difference between two recent model years of a popular domestic truck was the addition of a right-hand outside mirror.

There is one federal regulation which does give the buyer some protection. Section 1403, Volume 15, of the U.S. Code stipulates that car makers may be required to post the month and year of manufacture on the car's doorpost. More specifically, "the hinge pillar, the door latch post or the door edge that meets the door latch post next to the driver's side." However, this regulation has only been in effect since 1972. If your car is a 1972 model or later, it probably has that metal plate. If it's older, it probably won't.

Legal experts don't consider the regulation sufficient protection for consumers against model updating, however. In the first place, it only asks manufacturers to spell out when the car left the main assembly line, not what the *model year* is. Second, it does not help the man who buys a used car made before 1972. And third, few car buyers know about this regulation. Neither do most attorneys, consumer crusaders, or even DMV officials, simply because this is a federal regulation and its enforcement is up to federal agencies.

Manufacturers are fully aware of this law, and they are also aware that most consumers are not. One attorney says he has documents in his possession showing that one of Detroit's Big Three auto makers advised its dealers to inform buyers they were getting an updated vehicle only "if the purchaser questioned the difference between the model-year designation on the doorpost and the model-year designation under which the vehicle was being sold."

The obvious implication here is "buyer beware." And you have to be.

We have discussed in this chapter the most common frauds used across the country to gouge money from car owners. But more are being contrived almost daily. The best defenses are to stay with your car at an unfamiliar service station or garage, to get more than one estimate (and preferably three) in writing before letting anyone work on your car, and to have your regular mechanic (or one highly recommended) check your car thoroughly before beginning any trip.

These precautions are the cheapest and best insurance available against auto-repair fraud. Unfortunately, they are about the only ones.

Chapter 4

How Good
Is That Guarantee?

Possibly the single greatest improvement that could be made in the automotive service industry would be to abolish completely all warranties and parts guarantees.

But what about consumer protection? The truth is, these verbose and confusing documents that are supposed to assure customers of the quality of the product and the integrity of the manufacturers aren't worth a damn. The purpose of any service warranty or parts guarantee today is to limit the responsibility of the businessman. Despite advertising claims to the contrary, guarantees were never intended to protect consumers.

Without a guarantee or warranty, all product sales would fall under the implied warranty provision of the Uniform Commercial Code. This code is generally accepted for other industries and provides that a manufacturer must live up to all promises and stand behind his product even if it means *replacing it*. Wouldn't that be nice for the thousands of U.S. motorists each year who spend anywhere from $2000 to $10,000 or more for a new car and get stuck with a lemon. If, that is, auto makers really stood behind their product. But they know how to protect themselves.

Enter the new-car warranty designed to limit manufacturer and dealer responsibility. Each warranty generally starts off with a paragraph that goes something like this (italics ours).

"_____ warrants to the *original retail purchaser* that it will repair or replace, *at its option,* any parts of each new 19____

_____ passenger car vehicle and chassis (referred to as "vehicle"), including all equipment and accessories thereon (except tires) manufactured or supplied by _____, which are returned to an authorized _____ dealer at his place of business and which examination discloses to _____ reasonable satisfaction to be defective in material or workmanship under *normal use* and service. Such repairs and replacements shall be performed by such dealer without charge."

The trouble is, you're at the mercy of the people who made the car to decide if their product is defective or abused. Guess who holds the trump card in this relationship? And what happens if you, like most new-car buyers, pick out your dream machine after driving only a demonstrator model, return the next day to drive away in a new car you have probably never seen before, and then discover a dent in the door, a window that won't work properly, a door that's sprung, a heater that doesn't, or torn seat covers? If you are lucky and your dealer is conscientious, he may make things right for you. Then again, he may not. What recourse do you have? Legally, about zilch. You took delivery of the car without giving it a road test, and the warranty spells out quite clearly the limitations that free the manufacturer from completely guaranteeing his product. In fact, after the initial introductory paragraph quoted above, the remaining 90 percent or more of most new-car warranties is a listing of its limitations!

To wit:

"This warranty shall not apply to:

1. Normal maintenance services (such as engine tuneup, fuel-system cleaning, carbon or sludge removal, brake and clutch adjustments, and wheel alignment and balancing);
2. The replacement of service items (such as spark plugs, ignition points, positive crankcase ventilator valves, filters, and brake and clutch linings) made in connection with normal maintenance services;
3. Normal deterioration of soft trim and external appearance items due to wear and exposure;
4. The repair or replacement of any part, the failure of which is caused by lack of performance of required maintenance as specified by _____ in the 19____ New Vehicle Warranty and Owner Protection Plan folder attached.
5. Any part of a vehicle which has been subject to misuse, negligence, alteration, or accident so as in any way, in the

reasonable judgment of _____, to affect adversely its performance and reliability;

6. Any vehicle on which the odometer mileage has been altered and the vehicle's actual mileage cannot be readily determined;

7. Any vehicle for which the owner does not possess a _____ identification card issued in the owner's name; or

8. Any vehicle registered and normally operated outside the United States or Canada (the Warranty applicable to such vehicle shall be that authorized by _____ in the country where such vehicle is registered and normally operated).

At first all these loopholes and disclaimers sound fair. Until you read them over a couple of times and then realize that, with the manufacturer as both judge and jury as to *abuse vs. quality* and your footing the bill for all maintenance—*which the dealer must perform*—it doesn't take a legal genius to understand which party this document was designed to protect and favor. For example, if the engine is running sour, the wheels need balancing, or the front end needs alignment when you take delivery of the car, who pays the bill? The dealer? The manufacturer? Not on your life. Even though the car was obviously not in good tune or running condition when you took delivery, that kind of work falls clearly under the heading of "normal maintenance." It's spelled out in the contract.

Body bruises, flaws, and other damage, including flawed interior upholstery and workmanship, fit in the same category. If you didn't notice that small dent in the fender or that chrome strip that doesn't match or join properly with another, that's just too bad. Either get out your tools or your wallet, because neither the dealer nor the manufacturer is likely to fix those things free or give you another new car.

Some colorful efforts by unhappy car owners to get satisfaction have made headlines around the country in recent years, but they have resulted in little satisfaction otherwise. Eddie Campos doused his 1970 Lincoln with gasoline and set it on fire outside the Ford plant in Whittier, California. The trouble all started the first day Mr. Campos arrived home with his new car and his wife took it out for a drive. When she returned home and pulled the key out of the ignition, the entire assembly came out with it. His $6500 car went steadily, and expensively, downhill from there. Today the car sits in front of Mr. Campos' plastering business—with a tree growing out of its roof and a sign that says "If it's lemons you are going to buy, you might as well grow your own."

Owners of domestic cars do not have exclusive rights to such troubles. After repeated attempts to get his 1970 Toyota fixed, James Hammond burned it at the Shaefer and Strohmenger dealership in Baltimore where he had tried unsuccessfully for months to have problems corrected.

Such extreme tactics aren't recommended, but they do dramatically demonstrate just how frustrating new-car service can be and how far some customers are willing to go. Mr. Hammond did not win much understanding from the car manufacturer, but he did from the courts. A Baltimore judge let him off on probation after he was charged with disorderly conduct because of the burning incident.

"Instead of protesting the war, he protested against what he called inferior workmanship," the Associated Press quoted the judge as saying at the trial. "Apparently this thinking had built up in him until he had a cause."

Warranty limitations place a heavy burden on consumers to inspect carefully and road test any car they buy—before signing a sales contract, not on the way home. Just because a car is advertised as "new" doesn't mean it is in perfect condition or even good condition. One new-car service manager confided over drinks one evening that he doubted one out of nine cars sold at his dealership was really in top running condition, simply because nothing—except a quick wash—is done to them. No one, he said, from either the sales or service departments ever inspects or road tests a car, let alone performs such preparatory work as wheel alignment and balancing, engine tuneups, and a bit of bolt tightening here and there.

The reason for this lackadaisical attitude is simple economics in most cases. It would require one experienced (and highly paid) mechanic the better part of a regular working day to check one or two cars if they were really to be put in top shape. But an unskilled laborer, with a bucket of soapy water and some chrome cleaner, working for the minimum wage, can wash two or three cars an hour. Sitting on the showroom floor or out in the sunshine they look magnificent, yet experts estimate that every car leaves the factory with anywhere from five to 50 flaws in it. Since a quick wash job is all "dealer preparation" amounts to at many dealerships, buying a car is a gamble on whether you pick the one with only five flaws or the lemon with 50. And sometimes those five flaws can cause more trouble and expense than 50 lesser ones. Buying a car today is a risky business. The warranty doesn't make it much less risky.

This doesn't mean that factory warranties are worthless. In cases of major engine or transmission failure you are generally well protected—assuming you have fulfilled all maintenance requirements as detailed by the owner's manual. In all fairness to auto makers, this doesn't seem unreasonable since negligence is what brings mechanics about 80 percent of their business. (We will discuss automotive preventive medicine in a later chapter.) But since the motor and transmission are possibly the most reliable components in your car today, a warranty covering these seems less than generous! But at times it does, indeed, pay off.

Several years ago I bought a new MG during a tour of Europe. The car had about 10,000 miles on it when I headed for port to ship it back to the United States. But on the way a rod bearing let go. There wasn't time to have repairs made abroad, so I shipped it on to New York, gambling worriedly that I might get the trouble straightened out there. After picking up the car in Newark, I drove, clanking along noisily, into J. S. Inskip, a large British Leyland dealer in New York. I explained the situation and then held my breath, expecting to be turned away. To my pleasant surprise, however, I was told that the parts involved were defective; and the car was fixed free of charge two days later without hesitation or delay. In fact, they even rushed the car through when I mentioned that I couldn't spend more than a couple of days in the city.

I think this incident points out the value of carefully selecting your dealership. Regardless of who makes the car you buy, it is the dealership that determines how satisfied a customer you're going to be and it is to the dealership that you first turn if and when trouble strikes.

Another loophole in factory warranties that protects both the dealer and the maker is the statement acknowledging satisfaction with the condition of the car at the time of delivery. Almost all dealers have buyers sign this statement before taking delivery. Once this agreement has your signature on it, a dealer is perfectly within his rights, legally if not morally, to charge for any and all work not specifically covered by the manufacturer's rather limiting warranty. In a random poll of roughly a dozen experienced salesmen, not one could remember a customer who refused to sign this statement. When asked if they had ever had a prospective buyer who insisted on driving a new car before buying it, only one of them reported encountering such a demanding customer in more than 20 years of selling cars.

Why is that? Apparently because most car buyers don't seem to know much about cars and assume, for some naive reason, that a new car is in perfect condition. This despite all the publicity in recent years about factory recalls and the legions of irate customers like Campos and Hammond.

True, a good many automobile dealers around the country demand thorough preparation of their cars before delivery and spend the money necessary to offer that kind of service. But, like honest, well-trained mechanics, these are not the people we are concerned with in this book. Too many operations offer only the cursory preparation described; and then when you drive in the next day complaining, they expect you to pay for such things as brake adjustments, clutch adjustments, transmission adjustments, wheel balancing, front-end alignment, painting scratches, fixing faulty chrome fittings, repairing defective or torn upholstery, correcting wiring shorts, and on and on. All of these should have been checked out before the car was delivered and any problems corrected by the dealer. Even experts, however, can miss something. So, while any responsible dealer should fix these items gratis, few do.

There certainly is no reason why a new car cannot be delivered to you in perfect condition. If it isn't and the dealer doesn't want to correct the situation, it is a good indication that this outfit is much more interested in taking your money than in producing satisfied customers. Remember, a company that would sell a car to someone without making sure that vehicle is in top running condition is certainly not going to welcome you with smiles and open arms when you come around a few days later expecting to get things fixed on warranty.

Give yourself an edge from the very beginning. Talk with friends about the service received at the dealers where they bought their last cars. Try to find out which dealers are just as interested in producing satisfied customers as they are in record sales. Then make sure your new car is in near-perfect condition *before* signing any contracts. Don't rely on that warranty to set things straight later. It doesn't work that way in most places. If the car isn't in good condition when you road test it, insist that it be put in shape before you take delivery. Or, as an alternative, have the dealership put in writing on letterhead stationery exactly what will be fixed, adjusted, modified, or replaced *without charge* after you take delivery. This must be signed by the general manager—not the salesman or even sales manager, neither of whom carry that much weight. Remember, verbal agreements don't hold water in court. It won't do you any good to tell the judge, "But the salesman promised! . . ." Considering the nomadic nature of this business, the salesman you bought your car from yesterday may be selling sewing machines tomorrow.

Once you have selected the exact car you want to drive home, ask if you can take it out for a road test and tell the salesman that although he is more than welcome to come with you, you want to keep the car for at least an hour or two. It really doesn't matter whether he comes along or not, but he probably won't since he might make a sale during that time. But your offer should be both sincere and courteous.

How each dealership treats this request depends on how honest, reliable, and eager to satisfy customers it is. I have been flatly refused by some and others have suggested that I keep the car all day. Most car buyers look for the best money deal when they buy. It is much wiser to consider the integrity of the dealer, the overall quality of the car, and after-sale service. That doesn't mean that I dismiss the importance of trying to get the best deal. Just make sure you also include the other priorities.

You don't have to be a mechanic or race driver to conduct this simple new-car road test, which can save you considerable anxiety and expense later. It helps to carry a note pad and pen or pencil in case you begin finding things wrong and want to jot them down rather than trust your memory. If you have a friend who knows something about cars, invite him along. Generally speaking, however, it's best to hold the number of passengers down to one or two in order to keep noise and confusion at a minimum.

Now, away we go!

Drive the car for a few miles in busy city or stop-and-go traffic in order to check how smoothly and efficiently the brakes and transmission operate. This is also a good opportunity for you to check out such equipment as windshield wipers, heater, air conditioning, radio, power windows, power seats, and any other such gadgetry.

Then take the car out on the freeway to see how smoothly it rides. If you notice a bouncing or jerking in the steering it could mean that the wheels need balancing or the front end needs alignment. We should note that the manner in which new cars are transported (on trucks) often causes front-end alignment problems. This is fairly common, and it usually isn't serious enough for the average driver to notice. But the trouble shows up later—in the form of excessive or uneven tire wear. If you aren't sure you can diagnose the trouble, drop into a shop somewhere around town that specializes in alignment and get it checked out. The inspection shouldn't cost more than a couple of bucks and could save many times that amount later in return trips to the service department and in tire wear.

Next, inspect the body work carefully from several angles to see if there are any scratches, nicks, dings, or dents. This is one reason why it is always best to shop for a new car during the daylight hours. Then you can see what you buy much better.

Water leaks, especially around windows, can be maddening. To check for such leakage, drive home and run the hose over the car for about five minutes or stop by one of those do-it-yourself car washes.

This is where it helps to have someone with you. He can sit in the car while you spray water all over it. Few cars are absolutely watertight, so you have to be realistic. When you open the door after washing a car, water often rushes in, especially now that many makers have eliminated the rain gutter along the edges of the roof above the doors and windows. If you find any serious leaks you might just as well abandon that car in favor of another. Leaks and squeaks are among the most difficult problems to correct, so don't be too optimistic.

It's easy to complete this simple checkout ride in about an hour, usually in even less time. But don't rush, and don't feel guilty about it. A reliable dealer will have nothing to hide. Remember, no two cars are ever *exactly* alike. Taking a spin in a demonstrator may convince you that that specific model car is comfortable and nice to drive, but it tells you nothing about the quality and condition of the particular car you will drive home.

Equally important as the road test is reading the warranty and its accompanying maintenance manual, or whatever it is called by the manufacturer. Many new-car buyers either don't take the time to read these important documents or they gloss over them carelessly and then quickly find out they have inadvertently violated the service conditions. Most new-car warranties are contingent upon the owner's following a regular maintenance program. This required maintenance is reasonable, but some of the wording is vague and often misinterpreted by too many owners.

The most frequent trouble involves understanding the lubrication and oil-change requirements. Most warranties require this maintenance at varying mileage or time intervals—whichever comes first. That last phrase is what trips up most drivers. People seem to remember that the warranty says to get the oil changed every 6000 miles, but the part about "or every four months, whichever comes first" doesn't register. Since more than half of the cars in this country are driven less than 12,000 miles a year, there is a better than even chance that a motorist who waits until he racks up 6000 miles has technically violated the warranty if it has been more than four months since the last servicing. It's important then to watch the calendar as well as the odometer. Most reputable dealers will overlook these discrepancies, but you can't count on it. If you put up a fuss about the poor service or some trouble with the car, they might use the "breach of contract" to get rid of you. It happens every day.

But if new-car warranties are somewhat limiting and confusing, guarantees offered by some garages on repair work are literally worthless. These repair shops often advertise that all work is guaranteed. But when you ask them to spell out just what that guarantee includes, it usually translates to coverage of any parts used. That's not much of a guarantee, since most parts are already guaranteed against defects by the manufacturer. Even many of these parts guarantees are deceptive, because most of them are based on a pro rata system. This means that the replacement value diminishes the longer you use the part during the guarantee period. In other words, if a new battery costs you $30 and is guaranteed for one year, you will have to pay 50 percent or $15 to replace it if it goes on the blink in six months. Somehow, that doesn't seem like much of a warranty, especially since that battery or its equivalent may be on sale at some time for $15 or $20. On top of that, you are paying 50 percent more to get what you should have gotten in the first place!

The wording, also, of many guarantees is misleading. For example, the term "unconditional guarantee" is a misnomer, since all written guarantees by definition impose limits of some kind. Avoid being suckered into these tricks by reading all warranties carefully and shopping around before buying. The price of such items is often jacked up considerably to compensate for any potential losses the manufacturer or dealer might suffer through replacement.

A similar situation exists with the frequently used "50-50 guarantee" offered by many garages for repair work. The work is supposedly guaranteed for 30 days. During that time if anything goes wrong you split the cost of correcting it with the garage. In other words, you paid once to have the work done, but if the mechanic wasn't successful, he expects you to share the burden by subsidizing his incompetence. Not a bad deal at all for him! Adding to the absurdity of such guarantees is the fact that the mechanic can tell you the repairs cost twice what they actually did! You wind up paying the full amount (twice) instead of just half.

But there are indications that the federal government and some states are clamping down on abuses of the guarantee idea. After years of governmental studies, Congressional hearings, and mounting consumer outrage, Americans won a federal law that went into effect on

July 4, 1975, setting forth clearcut, tough standards on product warranties. This new law, known as the Magnuson-Moss Warranty-FTC (Federal Trade Commission) Improvements Act, doesn't compel manufacturers or retailers to offer warranties, but if they do, the warranties will have to say what they mean and mean what they say.

If companies or merchants do offer guarantees on products ranging from corkscrews to cars, the documents will have to state the terms and conditions of the guarantees in plain, easy-to-understand language, before the items involved are sold. If there is a breach of warranty, you are to have access to reasonable and effective remedies. And if there is a warranty, you are to be protected from sellers' disclaimers and "implied warranties"—pledges which may not be in writing but which imply that a product will operate as it is supposed to. Briefly, the law requires those who offer warranties to make explicit the following information:

> The party or parties to whom the warranty is extended;
> The product or parts covered and not covered by the warranty;
> An explanation of what the warrantor will do if the item is defective or breaks down and for what period of time and at whose expense;
> How long a warrantor will take to repair or replace a product or part once he is notified of its failure to meet the warranty standards;
> What we, as consumers, must do and what costs we must bear to obtain satisfaction from the warranty;
> A brief, general description of the informal as well as the legal remedies available to us when we dispute a warranty.

Under this law, any firm or store supplying a warranty must offer one of two types—a "full" warranty or a "limited" one. For a full warranty (you aren't likely to see any cars carrying one of these!) to be so designated, it must meet certain minimum federal standards included in the legislation. If you buy a battery that carries a full warranty, for instance, the company must repair or replace it promptly without charge once notified that it has gone on the blink. Also under the full warranty standards, the seller or manufacturer must refund the full purchase price or replace the faulty equipment if a "reasonable number" of attempts at repair have failed. The FTC will decide what constitutes a "reasonable number," and it will probably vary for different products. If a company decides to set a time limit on a full warranty, this fact must be made clear, so you are aware that the item is covered by a "full 90-day" or a "full three-year" warranty.

A full warranty must also apply to anyone who uses the product, not just to the original purchaser. If a warranty doesn't meet these standards, it is a "limited" warranty and must be conspicuously labeled as such. In addition, the law bans anyone who offers any type of full warranty from disclaiming or modifying "implied warranties," which often are unwritten but implied obligations owed to us, as buyers, by sellers and/or manufacturers. The law enables consumers who feel a warrantor has not complied with a written or implied warranty or service contract to bring suit in state or federal courts either individually or, under certain circumstances, as a class action, and to receive attorney fees.

Some states are also initiating laws to protect consumers from misleading warranties and those so full of loopholes and limitations that they prove worthless. California, for example, has passed a law imposing an implied warranty on any car sold, no matter how old, no matter how decrepit, no matter how cheap. The only way a dealer can void this warranty is to disclaim it at time of sale. As one veteran of the used-car lots remarked, " 'As is' just ain't what it used to be."

There are other new laws, equally obscure to the consumer but just as important to him, going on the books in many states. Many of these new laws will be given added strength under the federal consumer act described earlier. Following are some of the new consumer laws, many of which are not well known even in the legal profession.

A car buyer cannot be held to a deal if the dealer arranges for financing of the down payment and that loan falls through.

The buyer is not necessarily stuck with a lemon. There are two ways to get rid of the car if the dealer totally fails to live up to his obligations: The buyer can have the contract rescinded, or he can simply sell the car, even though he does not have clear title. Banks and finance companies are no longer disinterested bystanders in disputes arising from a sale. Lending institutions have been made subject to the same claims and defenses the buyer has against the dealer, as long as the financing was arranged through the dealer and the lending institution is one he uses regularly.

The buyer pays no attorney's fees or court costs if he brings suit against a dealer in a sales-contract dispute that provides for attorney's fees and wins. *The loser pays for both parties.*

These are among the laws regularly used by legal-aid and consumer lawyers, but otherwise generally unknown. They are not airtight, however. "It's a question of how far the law will go to cover a fool," says Charles M. Snell, a municipal court judge in San Diego. "No matter what the letter of the law, the key issue for the court is usually, 'What is reasonable?' "

In California, which, along with New York, Massachusetts, and Texas, seems to be setting the pace in consumer protection, implied warranties on used cars are good for three months when no express warranty exists. When an express (written) warranty is given with the car, the implied warranty statute still applies, but its duration is restricted to that of the express warranty. It shall, however, never be less than 30 days nor more than three months. In other words, the buyer who gets a written 15-day warranty is still protected for 15 more days by the implied warranty. If the written warranty is for a month or more, the implied warranty runs concurrently, up to a maximum of 90 days.

The law says that there is only one way a dealer can nullify the implied warranty. He must affix to the car "a conspicuous writing" which informs the buyer that (1) the car is being sold on an "as is" or "with all faults" basis, (2) the entire risk as to quality and performance rests with the buyer, and (3) the buyer assumes the entire cost of repairs. If a dealer has not disclaimed the implied warranty in this manner, it is presumed to be in effect. The "conspicuous writing" provision is an important one, according to consumer lawyer Philip D. Isaac.

"If you ask a dealer to make necessary repairs under the implied warranty and he points to some line in small print at the bottom of the sales contract which says 'as is,' it won't hold water," explains Isaac. "It has to be so conspicuous that no reasonably careful man can possibly miss it."

If you take legal action against a dealer you will need evidence in the form of either repair estimates by reputable repair shops or bills for repairs already made. According to judges, this second procedure is usually considered much stronger evidence than the mere presentation of estimates.

"If a man pays $500 out of his own pocket to fix a car, the court is much more likely to be inclined to believe that the repairs were really necessary," says Judge Snell. It must be emphasized, however, that the laws alluded to here are so complex and may vary considerably from state to state, that only a competent lawyer can make proper use of them. Some of the new consumer laws have not yet stood the test of appeal. Often a law that appears clear and unambiguous on paper is successfully challenged on the grounds that its legislative intent is not the same as its apparent meaning. But many of these state consumer protection laws will be given added strength by the Magnuson-Moss Act. Consumers in states where no such consumer protection is provided may find recourse in the federal law.

Thanks to the consumer revolt in this country, legal-aid organizations, lawyers, and some aggressive newspapers and other media, we buyers are winning new rights. But despite the growing protection now available, the primary responsibility for defending ourselves remains on our own shoulders. As the judge said, laws don't go far in protecting fools. Caution and good judgment should always be used before buying anything, especially something as expensive as a car. Be wary of the so-called "bargain" that may be a bargain only for the one who's unloading it. If you feel you didn't get a square deal, don't hesitate to consult with a consumer-protection group (there is a list in the back of this book) or a lawyer. Many companies are now finding out that their warranties must offer something valid to customers—especially tough customers.

Chapter 5

Where to Take a Sick Car

No matter how good the care you give your car is, it's almost certain to need expert attention at some time or another. Unless you're a skilled mechanic with a complete set of tools for the job, when that time comes you're apt to be faced with a confusing number of repair facilities to choose from. And you will not in the least be certain of how to make the best choice. This chapter is designed to reduce some of that confusion.

Maybe you number among that fortunate few who have already found a reliable mechanic. If so, count yourself lucky and skip this chapter altogether if you want. Most car owners, however, spend their entire motoring lives looking for a good mechanic who they are sure can be trusted to do a good job at a reasonable price. In order to give you some idea of where to look and what to look for, we are going to take you on a tour of the various kinds of repair facilities available in most areas and discuss the pros and cons of each.

As an outgrowth of the consumer revolt, many alternatives have been springing up throughout the country in the form of community and neighborhood health clinics, food cooperatives, and legal counseling. Although the idea has yet to spread to many other cities, the Cooperative Auto Shop of San Francisco, Inc., was organized in 1974 with the major premise that there is a need for a trustworthy means of repairing and maintaining cars at the lowest possible cost.

Amen!

When the co-op was incorporated in September of that year there were only seven members. Two months later the number was 80 with more applicants joining every day. Not surprising, is it? Members pay $20 a year, which entitles them to bring their car in for anything from an oil change to an engine overhaul at considerably reduced labor costs and cut-rate prices on parts.

The auto shop—like all co-ops—is owned by its members, who vote on the organization's policies. Lou Durham, a former Methodist clergyman who serves as the co-op's treasurer, explained that "as a cooperative our members would share in the profits, but the amount of return we anticipate is really very small. Our philosophy is that we would rather keep the prices of service down than try to make a return in the form of dividends.

"Although our corporate structure is similar to that of, say, a co-op food store, there is one major difference. Our auto shop isn't open to anyone but members. We're really an alternative business system."

The three men who do most of the work at the co-op auto shop's garage are guys who gave up better-paying jobs at other occupations because they enjoy working on cars and helping people. Allen Lohse, the co-op's secretary and shop manager, has a master's degree in social work from the University of Missouri. Donald Mincks, co-manager, spent three years as a real-estate loan officer for a major bank and did title insurance and escrow work before that. Al Wendgerd, whose corporate title is "grease monkey," spent five years as a computer operator. All three got into the co-op because working on cars was their hobby.

The $20 membership fee at the co-op entitles members to service at the rate of $15 an hour for labor and a discount on parts.

"Some dealer shops charge as much as $35 an hour for labor," Lohse said. "The average repair shop charges $20 to $25 an hour. There are one-man shops here and there that charge the same or even less than we do. But we figure our price is fair because we're giving customers an ingredient that isn't always easy to find—honesty.

"If we don't know the answer, we say so. If it's a job we can't do, we say so. There are things we can't do. For transmission work, or heavy engine work, welding or body work, we've found places we've checked out that are reliable and honest. We refer people to them.

"All in all, I figure we save our customers about one-third of what car repairs might normally cost them—and lots more than that if they had gone to a place that was looking to take them."

The co-op mechanics are paid only $2 an hour, they said, because most of the revenue goes for rent and equipment. Eventually, they hope, wages will improve as membership grows and initial expenses are absorbed. But their motives are hardly mercenary.

"I worked in a station once as a mechanic," Wendgerd says. "It was years ago. I replaced two feet of wire in a car one day and the boss charged the customer $200. He told him we had to replace the whole wiring system. The guy paid it without a question. Well, I never forgot that."

Unfortunately, few car owners have auto-repair co-ops available to them. So for those depending on the more conventional facilities, we're going to take a close look at what each has to offer you and your car.

New-Car Dealerships

The quality of work you're apt to encounter here ranges from the best available to the sloppiest and most frustrating and expensive.

It all depends on the operation. You won't be able to tell the difference by just walking in, so you'll have to do a little detective work on your own.

Car companies are in the business of selling cars, not repairing them. That message comes through loud and clear from the factory. Technically the dealer is an independent businessman who contracts to sell and service the manufacturer's product, but the emphasis is on the selling. Dealers do not receive an exclusive franchise for a specified territory to limit competition, as is the case in most other franchised businesses such as quick-food operations.

A new-car dealer must stock parts and provide service to customers. But he also promises to meet a minimum sales quota *set by the manufacturer,* and if he doesn't meet this quota the franchise is subject to cancellation.

The auto maker's major concern is always sales, because 90 percent of its income is from new-car sales and only 10 percent is from the sale of parts in connection with service. Auto companies often cancel dealer franchises for failing to meet sales quotas, but rarely, if ever, do they can a dealer for not providing adequate service facilities or for poor repair work.

Dealers therefore are pressured into emphasizing sales and view service and repair work as necessary evils. Dealerships and individual sales personnel are often rewarded with bonuses for superior sales performance, but there is rarely any like reward for outstanding service. It wasn't always so. What led to this situation?

As new-car production lines became more and more automated,

particularly following World War II, new cars began rolling out factory doors in record numbers. Dealerships suddenly found themselves with more cars than customers. Detroit had the answer in one powerful word: *volume*. Why sit around waiting for one customer to give you $500 profit on one car, when you can double or even triple sales by clearing only, say, $200 a car, but with customers lining up by the thousands to get in on the bargain!

The idea obviously caught on. Today we're told and sold the virtues of high-volume business. Which is fine as long as it doesn't interfere with product quality and service. But it does. And that explains why it often takes a week or two at many dealerships to get an appointment just to have the oil changed in your shiny new Chromemobile.

The average profit dealers enjoy on each car is about two percent, with a top of around five percent. If you know anything about business you know that such a profit margin is ridiculously small. If you don't know a thing about business you probably guessed as much. For example, the markup on merchandise like clothing and jewelry ranges from 50 to 150 percent or more.

So how does the new-car dealership stay in business then? And pay for all those bright lights, television and newspaper ads, office and sales staff, and a service department? It's not easy. But here's a clue. Americans spend roughly $30 billion a year on new cars. They also spend roughly the same amount each year on service and repair.

Public opinion reflects the situation quite graphically. Several years ago, pollster George Gallup made a nationwide survey to find out how people rated seven occupational groups: new-car dealers, bankers, druggists, supermarket managers, undertakers, service-station managers, and plumbers. Interviewees were asked to rank these businessmen in terms of how honest and trustworthy they are. Only three percent of those surveyed considered new-car dealers to be honest and trustworthy. In another survey, advertising executive David Ogilvy found that only 38 percent of car owners went to the dealer for service or repair because most of them considered dealers untrustworthy, their prices too high, and the waits too long.

But is it really the dealer's fault? No. Not entirely, at least. Dealers generally don't like to perform warranty work because they get only slightly more than a wholesale price on parts from the manufacturer and less on labor charges than they would get from a paying customer. Adding insult to injury is the fact that auto makers are woefully slow in making payment. Because of such little profit on both parts and labor, mechanics working at dealerships are forced to resort to quick work and a great deal of parts changing. They don't have time to spend four hours repairing a faulty fuel pump, for example, when they can replace the defective part with a new one in 30 minutes and make twice the money. It's good business for dealers and mechanics, but not for you and me.

What this means, of course, is that fewer and fewer dealers across the country are interested in providing after-sale service of any kind on warranty. It also means that you're apt to pay more for nonwarranty work because dealers try to make up for the little profit they earn when working for the factory. Booz Allen & Hamilton, Inc., one of the largest management consultant groups in the country, reported in a study conducted for the Department of Transportation that dealers frequently perform phony repairs, charge for new parts when used ones are installed, put down more labor time than the repair actually requires, overcharge for parts, and engage in many other clever little deceits at the customer's expense.

Many dealers don't pretend the situation is otherwise. Nor do they like it that way. "We as dealers are not satisfied and do not feel that we are being properly compensated through the use of the warranty formula used by the various manufacturers," is what T. A. Williams, president of the National Automobile Dealers Association, told the Senate Subcommittee on Antitrust and Monopoly. "This is part of the reason why there is a difference in some dealerships between a warranty rate and a customer rate."

The mechanic too is caught in this web of slim profit and big volume. He can either adapt to it by rationalizing the situation as a natural result of the free-enterprise system or look elsewhere for employment. Every possible adjustment, replacement, and repair is indexed and given a time allowance in each manufacturer's flat-rate book. Each operation, whether changing spark plugs or replacing the engine head gasket, is allocated an exact amount of time in hours and tenths of an hour. Thus, 1.5 hours translates to one hour and 30 minutes, while 0.6 hours equals 36 minutes. If the hourly flat rate at a dealership is $20 an hour and a certain job is listed as requiring 1.5 hours, it's going to cost the customer $30 for labor alone—even if the mechanic can perform the job in half that time.

Most mechanics can beat the flat-rate time easily, which may explain why so many mechanics complete 15 hours of service labor each day though they are only in the shop for eight hours! Believe me, that's the rule rather than the exception. With mechanics receiving anywhere from 40 to 60 percent on all labor costs and parts, that stacks up as a tidy profit margin on service for both repairmen and dealer. The secret is to run cars through as quickly as possible. The result is assemblyline-style service which has become all too synonymous with poor quality and dissatisfaction among motorists. Many auto-industry critics also deplore the flat-rate system as nothing short of blatant price fixing—an ironic situation, it seems, in an industry so bitterly competitive in every other respect.

As you enter the dealership service department you will be greeted by a man wearing a smile and a white knee-length smock, and carrying a clipboard. Contrary to popular myth, this guy is not a senior service expert, veteran mechanic, engineering whiz, or even a diagnostic robot. At about nine out of ten new-car dealers he is a service *salesman* only. He may even know a lot less about cars than you do. His job is to get as much business in and out in a work day as possible. The better he does this, the more secure is his job. The personnel turnover in this field is even higher than among car salesmen, as you no doubt have noticed if you've visited one dealership with any frequency.

New-car service departments are often impressive with their numer-ous service stalls and racks, their expensive and elaborate equipment, and the bustle of activity always found in such shops. You will find specialization carried to a greater degree here than at most garages. There are specialists in air conditioning, tuneup, alignment, and transmission repair—all under one roof. The cost of service or any kind of repair here is apt to be higher than at other garages for several reasons. First, the warranty versus nonwarranty work forces most dealers to charge their paying customers more than an independent shop. Second, you're going to pay more for "brand name parts and service"—which means the name of a manufacturer over the door and the notion that you're dealing with "factory trained mechanics," which you now know is so much baloney. Third, because of the high volume of repair work, you encounter more parts changing than elsewhere. You can expect a dealership mechanic to begin pulling new replace-ment parts off the shelves before he has even attempted to diagnose the trouble and carefully inspect the old parts involved.

You'll find that the quality of work varies considerably. It all depends on the ethics of the people who run the place and the luck of the draw as to which mechanic works on your car. Your best bet is to do some checking around before driving in and turning your new car over to these people. Ask around—where you work, in the neighbor-hood, among friends—to find out if anyone has dealt with this establishment. Never authorize nonwarranty repairs at a dealer until you have shopped around at two or three places. Be especially careful when you have your car in a shop for warranty maintenance. That's when mechanics are likely to look around for nonwarranty repairs to pad the bill—and their wallets.

Considering these drawbacks, is there any reason for patronizing new-car dealer service departments for anything beyond routine maintenance covered by warranty? Yes. You can avoid much of the usual trouble ahead of time by checking out the car you buy before you buy and determining how easy and inexpensive it will be to service and repair later. According to Ralph Nader, much of the cost of auto repair could be reduced or even eliminated altogether "if key parts were not so inaccessible or fragile, or so constructed that a small defect requires replacement of an entire large unit of the car."

The more luxuries and gadgets on a car (hidden headlights, power-assisted equipment such as windows, seats, antennas, and steering, and all high-performance options), the more likely it is to need frequent repairs, and the more those repairs are apt to cost.

Although mechanics at dealer service shops are unlikely to be any more skilled than other members of their trade, they are often more familiar with the problems of the particular make of car they work on. In some instances, this could save you both time and money. That should be a consideration. Dealerships also may be your safest bet for service or repair work when you are traveling and are totally unfamiliar with any other repair facilities.

Mass Merchandisers and Franchised Specialty Shops

When it comes to fried chicken and hamburgers, the franchise idea works well enough. It offers mediocre food at reasonable prices. When you buy a bucket of chicken or a double-deck hamburger from one of these operations in Los Angeles or Miami Beach, you know it's always going to taste the same. It's quick and easy dining. Quality control is easy, and just about anyone can learn to wash his hands and fry chicken or hamburgers with minimal instruction and practice. But you should demand a little more expertise than that when someone has to fix the brakes on your car.

Just as a top chef is unlikely to be found salting French fries behind the counter of your local short-order diner, a top mechanic probably isn't going to take his skills to a place that specializes in selling and installing tires or mufflers. Emphasis should be placed on the word *selling* in this case. Over the past two decades shrewd businessmen seasoned in the ways of marketing and mass merchandising have discovered gold in automotive parts and service. Anyone who watches a few hours of television each week or visits suburban shopping centers is well aware that even department stores, which once specialized almost exclusively in home furnishings and wearing apparel, now offer everything in the way of automotive service—from tires to tuneups. In some cases, auto parts and service now accounts for a full five percent of their total business. A hefty chunk of money.

There are at least a dozen mass merchandisers across the country who have turned their buying and selling power and marketing expertise into a successful auto parts and service sideline; the list includes Sears, Roebuck and Company; Montgomery Ward; K-Mart; J. C. Penney; S. S. Kresge; and E. J. Korvette.

Expert at merchandising and able to buy parts in volume at low prices, these business giants have quickly gained ground on independent garages and even new-car dealerships by offering fast and convenient service at low rates. Indeed they can offer customers real bargains. The bulk of their work—and profit—comes from selling replacement items (batteries, tires, shock absorbers, and mufflers) and offering quick service (brake jobs and wheel balancing).

Their considerable success is based on established reputation, heavy advertising, convenience, and low prices. But don't be seduced by any of those factors. To be sure, it's convenient to drop off your car at one of these service centers, spend the morning or afternoon shopping, return to pick it up, and have the bill charged to your account. Because these big operations buy and sell auto parts and accessories in such tremendous volume they can offer you lower prices than you'll find at many other places. But you must be aware that the so-called mechanics at these shops are only thinly veiled salesmen, and they aren't likely to let you get in and out with only a change of rubber or shocks if they can help it. With a little verbal arm twisting and double talk they will try to convince you to opt for a better grade of tire (also more expensive) or additional (and often unneeded) work that will add to your bill—and their commissions.

You'll find a similar situation at the specialty shops, which lure you through their doors with bargain claims on tires, mufflers, or transmission repairs. But they have no intention of letting you leave without spending a great deal more than you figured on when you drove in.

The ethics involved here are certainly questionable. But the facts are not. If you are wise enough to capitalize on the low prices of some parts and accessories, and even service sometimes, it can be worth your while. Just keep in mind that low prices and quick service do not necessarily mean quality material and workmanship. Americans have become accustomed to franchise operations as a standard of quality—however mediocre. We tend to trust this kind of business enterprise and use it as a standard, assuming that the reason large companies are growing and making money is the result of hard work, honesty, integrity, and quality. But any business thrives and grows as a result of intelligent marketing and management, combined with aggressive and creative advertising. The quality of service and product need not be outstanding, it must only be satisfactory to the greatest number of customers. Since few people are sophisticated in matters of either food or automobiles, the standard does not have to be very high.

That can change. You're proving that right now by reading this book. People may not always know how or where to find quality merchandise, but we think most of them want to find out. Like you. If you know exactly what is wrong with your car, you can often save time and money by taking it to one of the mass merchandisers or specialty shops. Just don't let them talk you into unnecessary expenditures. Get a second or third opinion. These shops can do a job, such as installing a muffler or new tires, cheaper because that's their specialty and the employees are adept at doing what they do because they do it over and over all day every day. But that doesn't mean that the guy who fits new tires on your car is capable at brake work or tune-ups.

Nor is that famous name over the door of many specialty shops necessarily an endorsement of high quality. The franchised name is sold to anyone who has the money to go into business and agrees to use the parent company's products. The parent company rarely polices the activities of its franchised outlets (especially as long as business is good) or trains the employees. So you will always have to investigate each shop independently, just as you would a service station or independent garage, despite frequent advertising claims that "each branch maintains the same high quality."

Specialty shops and mass merchandisers are frequently guilty of the bait-and-switch ploy to attract customers. They will advertise such things as $9.95 tune-ups, failing to explain that that only includes parts—not labor, which will probably boost the total bill to around $30.

There have been some feeble attempts by consumer groups and even the government to protect car owners from such ethics, but with limited success. Both AAMCO, the transmission specialists, and Midas, the muffler experts, have been slapped on the wrists by the Federal Trade Commission for false or misleading advertising claims falling into the bait-and-switch category. These are certainly not small fly-by-night operations, they are rather multimillion-dollar corporations doing business in almost every part of the country.

The FTC charged AAMCO with deception as its "plan or method of doing business"—by offering free diagnoses. When customers drove in, according to the FTC, they were told the trouble could only be diagnosed by removing, dismantling, and inspecting the transmission— all free of charge. But, after the transmission was disassembled, if the customer decided not to have it repaired there, AAMCO would refuse to put it back together and replace it in the car.

"The sole object of this procedure is to persuade and induce the customer to transfer custody of his automobile to the AAMCO shop so that he may be subjected to efforts to sell him an 'AAMCO custom rebuilt' transmission or other products or services at prices greatly in excess of the low prices offered in the advertisements," the FTC complaint said. The FTC concluded that AAMCO deprived customers of the opportunity to freely choose the services they needed.

A similar complaint was issued by the FTC against Midas and its franchise operators, citing misleading advertising. The muffler firm was chastised for claiming "You can keep your car forever and never have to buy another muffler. That's what the Midas guarantee means. Guarantee—no charge for installation, it's free! Nothing evasive. No fine print double-talk. It says 'guaranteed for the life of your car.'" Midas, however, charged return customers for service despite its advertising claims. The company still bases much of its advertising on the slogan "guaranteed for as long as you own your car," but it now mentions the installation charge.

In June 1970, the FTC ordered AAMCO to halt its allegedly deceptive advertising practices and issued 18 points for compliance. Since then the FTC has continued to be inundated with complaints but reports only that it is so understaffed and low on funds that it cannot, in fact, hope to force the issue or take the corporation to court. Meanwhile, AAMCO has changed its ad campaign in order to attract customers by emphasizing its extensive experience with all kinds of transmissions instead of promises of free examinations.

AAMCO and Midas are big targets and have the resources to reach many car owners, but they are not the only specialty outfits whose business ethics have been questioned. Many smaller, lesser-known firms operating throughout the country on a local or regional level employ all manner of tactics to attract the unwary. Even apart from bait-and-switch techniques, customers often have a difficult time resisting the hard sell they encounter. So be prepared.

The growing number of auto-accessory shops throughout the country is a good example. There are an estimated 25,000 of them, and many are franchised by such tire manufacturers as Goodyear, Firestone, General Tire, and B. F. Goodrich. They often advertise free wheel balancing and alignment with each set of new tires. This kind of offer can be worthwhile only if you resist the hard sell to buy more expensive tires that are not on sale and the multitude of other accessories or services they may try to convince you are necessary.

Please remember this: With the exception of brake repair, worn tires, and a dead battery, few service needs are ever urgent. If the tires are bald or the battery's dead, you'll know it. And it is a rare situation when brake repairs won't wait long enough for you to shop around and get several opinions.

Our best recommendation regarding mass merchandisers, specialty, and accessory shops is to take advantage of their convenience and sometime bargain prices when you can. But always shop with caution and be prepared to resist aggressive and expert salesmanship. Too often these people are more interested in your money than your welfare—or your car's.

Service Stations

Service stations used to be places where you stopped in for gas, had the water and oil checked, and the windshield washed (however much of a mess the attendant made of it). Today, however, many stations perform extensive auto repair. And the quality of that repair varies widely. The obvious attraction for car owners is usually convenience and accessibility. In most cities you only have to drive a block or two to find a gas station. Most of them are open late at night and on weekends, and if you need a new tire or an engine tune-up, you can charge it on your credit card.

There are nearly a quarter of a million service stations in this country, and they account for roughly 20 percent of all auto-repair business. The problem is distinguishing between the ones employing good mechanics capable of fixing your car and those performing repairs strictly to earn extra money and to keep attendants busy when they aren't pumping gas and washing windshields. Many times the attendant with the most tenure is handed the post of "mechanic," even though his only experience has been pumping gas and changing wiper blades, oil, and spark plugs. This fellow won't be working on your car, he'll be practicing on it and charging you for his schooling. A real bargain for him, but not much of a deal for you.

Cars are complicated. Hanging around a gas station and performing lubrications, oil changes, and installing new parts and accessories doesn't qualify anyone for the job of mechanic. But that's the way it works much of the time. Most stations performing repair work do it strictly as a sideline. In some small towns and rural areas you can still find the "garage station"—a vanishing species of independent garage employing a kid part time to pump gas while the mechanics tend to their specialties. They are usually outstanding. More than 90 percent of the service stations you will encounter, however, are in the business to sell gas and peddle the parent company's tires and batteries. They normally don't even stock many other parts except for spark plugs and oil filters.

Perhaps the biggest weakness of the service station as a reliable auto-repair facility is the limited equipment it has available to both diagnose and correct malfunctions. Nor do the men who work there see any one particular problem in any make of car often enough to become expert at fixing it. Think about it. How many times have service station attendants asked you where the gas cap is located or how to open the hood? Is this the guy you would trust to repair your brakes or tune your engine? Hardly. But for most car owners the attendant and the mechanic are one and the same. How would you react if you visited a doctor and complained to him of, say, a sore throat and he asked you to show him where it hurt? Maybe the analogy seems a little far out, but I think in either case you've picked a loser. Drive down the street and look for someone else.

Generally, service stations located in cities or towns and away from the main streets, boulevards, and highways are more likely to offer good repair work, since they probably cater more to regular customers and rely more heavily on repeat business than they do on selling gas and accessories. In contrast, those located along the freeways and at busy intersections are more likely to specialize in peddling accessories and pumping gas and offer repairs only as a sideline. Keep in mind, however, that there are certainly exceptions in both cases.

Parts at service stations usually cost as much or more than they would if you walked in off the street and bought what you needed at an auto-parts store. So don't expect any bargains unless you are a regular customer and know the man you're dealing with. He might then give you a reduced rate on parts, which, you must remember, cuts into his own profit. Labor rates, however, are frequently lower than anyplace else, primarily because overhead costs are absorbed some by the sale of gasoline, oil, and minor accessories. Keep in mind the fact that most (but certainly not all) service station mechanics are not what you might call tops in their trade. Many good mechanics do, however, run service stations and employ attendants to handle the light work while they themselves keep busy repairing cars. If you run across this kind of operation, especially near where you live, don't hesitate to take advantage of it. We're not trying to scare you away from using service stations for repairs; we are only pointing out their limitations and advising car owners to be cautious. For minor repairs and regular maintenance needs the corner gas station may be your best bet, particularly when all you need is a tune-up, lube job, oil change, or new battery. But I'd leave all heavy and tricky work, especially involving the carburetor, brakes, and transmission, and any engine work requiring removal of the heads, to experts.

Perhaps the single biggest advantage to dealing with your local service station for all or most of your automotive needs is that, like the family doctor, your man at the pumps sees your car regularly. If he is a reliable mechanic and is interested in you as a regular customer, he can often spot trouble long before it develops into something more serious and *expensive.* Even if he doesn't have the knowledge or equipment to make a particular repair, he may advise you of what is necessary and recommend a place to have it done. That kind of professional advice is just about priceless.

Independent Garages

Like those nostalgic mom 'n' pop grocery stores and drugstore soda fountains, the independent garage appears headed for extinction. They are, to be sure, on the decline, and that's really too bad for many reasons. It limits business opportunities for enterprising and ambitious mechanics, and it reduces the chances car owners around the country have of finding good and inexpensive auto repairs. There are approximately 110,000 independent garages today in the United States, compared with more than some 150,000 only a decade ago.

Apparently causing this decline in the number of independent operators are the inroads in the auto-repair business being made by the mass merchandisers and accessory and specialty shops. Independent garage owners are finding it difficult at best, and often impossible, to compete with the heavy advertising and cut-rate prices that their big-money colleagues are able to employ to attract business. Many motorists, fed up with the lack of standards in the auto-repair industry, are relying on the more-established firms and franchise operations in hopes of finding at least some level of reliability, however mediocre.

The independents must rely almost exclusively on quality workmanship and reasonable prices in order to encourage repeat business and, hopefully, some word-of-mouth advertising, which is about the only kind they can afford. It is for these reasons that your best bet for solid and relatively inexpensive auto repair is the small one- or two-man independent garage. Your second choice should be the larger independent operations which often resemble new-car dealerships because of their numerous repair and service stalls, hoists, and the often exotic and sophisticated diagnostic equipment. Here you will find specialists in brake and transmission repair, tune-ups, and sometimes even major engine repair. Labor rates are apt to be high, but so is the quality and standard of work.

Independent garage owners are in business for one reason only—to repair cars. They are not mere fronts for selling accessories or gas. Few among them, even the largest, can afford bad publicity or expensive advertising in order to attract new customers. Most of them do not rely on the flat-rate system for labor charges, which means you're more likely to pay less, especially at the smaller shops. Higher labor rates, if any, might well be offset by honesty and quick work, and possibly a reduced cost on parts since the larger independent operators often deal directly with the manufacturer. Equally important, many of these shops actually *repair* broken parts instead of automatically tossing them in the trash and installing new replacements.

The independent garage owner is a small businessman who has probably worked hard to build a regular clientele. He has built his business (unless it happens to be the only one in town) through hard work, honesty, personalized service, and, quite often, lower labor rates than the big franchised operations. The owner at a small shop may well crawl out from under a car when you enter, wipe off his hands, and ask with a smile if there's anything he can do to help you. He means that. His budget, overhead, and profit margin are all likely to be small. Very small. He takes pride in his work—in a way no new-car dealership mechanic, muffler installer, or tire changer could ever imagine. That enthusiasm rubs off on you in several ways. It makes the entire business of getting your car fixed a little less unpleasant, and it improves your chances of getting satisfactory service for a reasonable amount of money.

Even the large independent shops, which often make some new-car service departments look inadequate by comparison, can offer more personal service than you are apt to encounter at the big franchise operations or dealerships. Although the owner of this kind of shop is more likely to appear in a white shirt and tie and carrying a pen than in overalls and holding a wrench, he still probably has a paternal feeling about the operation, selects his employees carefully, and supervises their work closely. You won't feel you are getting as much personalized service here as at the small shops, but there is certainly great comfort in knowing that the buck stops with the guy you talked to this morning instead of some slick-tongued stranger in another city or state. The man you deal with at most independent garages will be genuinely glad you stopped in. And in most cases you will be too.

If you aren't entirely satisfied with the service you get from an independent operator, your chances of getting results when you complain are better than they are at almost any other kind of auto-repair facility, with the possible exception of a reliable neighborhood service station. Notice that we qualify that, because not all gas station operators or the parent oil company are interested in customer complaints, despite their frequent and eloquent lip service to the contrary.

It is also at the independent shop that you are most likely to deal with a real mechanic who can make repairs that save you money. This is where "R & R" on the work order means remove and *repair,* not remove and *replace.*

The simple solenoid switch is a good example of the parts-changing syndrome so rampant today in so-called repair shops. This tiny switch is a small wired coil that creates a strong magnetic field whenever the ignition key is turned. Simply stated, it acts as a bridge to bring current from the battery to the starter motor. (See dictionary of automotive terms in the back of this book.) The actual contact is a small round washer made of either brass or copper. When you consider how often you start your car, it's easy to imagine what a workout this little magnet gets in the course of two or three years. The side of the washer that actually makes the contact gradually becomes pitted. Then one day you turn the key and hear only a frustrating "click." This means there is no longer enough smooth surface on the washer to make a connection. Many mechanics (we should probably put that word in quotes about half the time we use it!) will quickly replace the "worn out" solenoid with a new one and charge you somewhere between $10 and $30, depending on the type of car. But if you are lucky enough to have found a genuine *mechanic* or repairman, he will probably simply remove that little washer and replace it with a new one, or, better yet, he will turn it around so the opposite side, which is still smooth, can make contact. The charge for this service should be somewhere between nothing and about $3. If you pay more than that, you're being overcharged. Make a fuss so the guy knows you aren't a fool. However, anyone who knows enough to make this kind of repair isn't likely to try and gouge you. If he were going to do that, he would merely have installed a new—and unnecessary—part.

Let's consider one more example of how a real mechanic can save you time and money. The distributor, which delivers electrical current to the spark plugs, is a frequent source of trouble. But this problem is usually quick, easy, and inexpensive to correct. Because of constant changes in temperature, the distributor cap—an item costing from $3 to $5 for most domestic cars—sometimes cracks, allowing dirt and moisture to get inside. The result is an annoying misfiring that grows gradually worse until the engine won't run at all. A salesman disguised as a mechanic-cum-parts-changer will sell the gullible motorist a new distributor for anywhere from $18 to about $28, when in most cases only a new cap would be more than sufficient to end the problem permanently.

Of course, a really good, old-fashioned repairman could do even better. Instead of replacing the cap, he might well perform a backyard garage trick I learned years ago when I was rebuilding aging clunkers and turning them into what I thought were magnificent street racers. Since the budget was badly limited in those days (funny how things don't always change that much over the years!), a great deal of imaginative field expediency—as they call it in the military—was necessary. Simply remove the cap, wipe it clean, and drill a small hole in the top to allow the moisture to escape and the cap to dry out, eliminating the buildup of crud. You may, of course, have to wipe out dirt and grime every month or so. But otherwise this kind of home repair can suffice indefinitely, requiring only about five minutes and saving you anywhere from $15 to $30.

These are just two examples culled from among the literally dozens of small and inexpensive repairs a mechanic who knows his trade can perform in order to save his customers time and money—if he wants to.

Your best chance of finding this kind of chap is always at the small independent shop or at your neighborhood service station.

Every auto-repair facility has its own special limitations, however. The small shop is no exception. Only you can weigh these limitations in relation to your special needs. For example, small independents rarely stock a large selection of parts, and they may have trouble finding the parts they don't have on hand. This could mean some delay in the repair of your car. If the small garage has a fine reputation, it will probably be busy, with possibly a backlog of work. This means you may have to make an appointment several days or even weeks in advance, which certainly can be more than a minor inconvenience if the trouble is serious.

Although some of the larger independent shops may have diagnostic equipment, few of the small ones can afford such an investment. Thus, both you and the mechanic are dependent strictly upon his trouble-shooting skills to locate and correct the problem, at times tricky and difficult even for experts. A wrong judgment could result in expensive and unnecessary repairs, requiring a return visit. This, however, is most unlikely if you are dealing with a reliable shop. It may take a little longer to isolate the trouble, but what you may lose in time you'll probably gain in skill and thoroughness—and possibly in money-saving techniques such as those described previously.

Perhaps the biggest difficulty in dealing with the independents is finding one you can trust. If none of your friends are able to steer you to someone, check around at some of those small used-car lots—the ones specializing in sharp-looking older models. Most of these places send their work out. So, if there is a mechanical wizard in the area, they're sure to know who he is.

Accepting the drawbacks and limitations, the small- to medium-sized independent garage is a good bet for honest and competent auto repair at a reasonable price. Just don't rush in blindly.

Diagnostic Centers

When diagnostic centers first began springing up in cities across the country in the mid-60s, they were lauded by many as the greatest boon to auto repair since the socket wrench or the pneumatic hoist.

That enthusiasm cooled somewhat, however, when many car owners quickly discovered that diagnostic centers and their elaborate equipment were only as reliable as the people who ran them. In many cases that wasn't much of a recommendation.

Unfortunately, the situation isn't much better today. In theory, you should be able to drive into one of these Mayo Clinics of the auto-repair industry, turn your car over to some white-coated specialist who will put it through extensive tests via sophisticated diagnostic computers, and find out just what, if anything, is ailing it. All that for a nominal fee ranging from $10 to about $30. You, in turn, can then decide whether to have your buggy put back in good health or get rid of it—if the cost of repair is prohibitive.

In practice, however, it doesn't always work quite that smoothly and simply. Many of these centers are merely fronts for repair facilities, relying on their impressive appearance to con car owners into unnecessary repairs. Diagnostic-center operators often started out with good intentions, but they quickly discovered that the only way to make money was to open a repair shop next door and to send it a lot of business. This can be okay if you're dealing with honest folk. But it smacks of unhealthy patronage, and you should be especially cautious in dealing with this kind of setup. There are a few independent diagnostic centers around the country that are not affiliated with any repair facility. Count yourself lucky if one is located in your area. (We have compiled a list of the known independents at the end of this chapter.)

Diagnostic centers can be of particular value if you want to give your car a thorough physical just before the warranty expires or before leaving on a motor trip. The same holds true when you are interested in buying a used car that looks great but aren't sure just how good it is underneath the hood; or if your own car sounds and acts like it's breathing its last, and you don't know whether to junk it or get it fixed.

Diagnostic centers have tremendous potential in helping car owners to get the most out of their repair dollars and to avoid major repairs altogether by spotting trouble before it becomes serious. If Senator Hart has his way, a network of independent diagnostic centers will be established across the country where, for a few dollars, you will be able to find out what repairs, if any, are needed for your car. After you have the repairs made elsewhere, you can then return to the diagnostic center to see how well the work was performed.

One organization that has had some experience in the diagnostic field is the American Automobile Association (AAA) and its affiliates. Nonprofit diagnostic clinics are run by the California State Auto Association Clubs in San Francisco and the Automobile Club of Missouri in St. Louis. The Automobile Club of Southern California has signed contracts with 16 diagnostic clinics that have met its criteria and recommends them to its members. Always keep in mind, however, that a diagnostic center must have certain equipment in order to truly qualify as a legitimate diagnostic center. Otherwise it is nothing more than a run-of-the-mill repair shop. One of the most important pieces of necessary equipment is the dynamometer. This is an expensive machine that simulates various driving and road conditions in order to test and analyze your car's health. The car's wheels simply rest on the dynamometer's rollers; the machine then creates various road conditions, such as turning, accelerating, braking, and climbing hills at speeds of up to 70 mph. Meanwhile, other diagnostic equipment is hooked up to your car to record how well it is doing. If something isn't performing the way it should, the instruments will pinpoint the trouble.

In addition to a dynamometer, a good diagnostic center should also have the following:

Brake analyzer to test the front and rear brakes under actual driving speeds

Oscilloscope to check timing, carburetion, ignition points, and spark plugs

Hydrocarbon and carbon monoxide meter to check emissions (also to locate a carburetion or ignition problem)

Rack or hoist to raise the vehicle for inspection of its undercarriage

Equipment to check front-end alignment

Equipment to check headlights

Jim McDowell, director of national emergency road service for the AAA, warns consumers not to be awed by exotic-looking diagnostic equipment. "Most of the equipment out today is dependent upon the mechanic," McDowell explains. "The most important aspect of a good diagnosis is the man himself."

Generally, experts advise car owners to ask about the mechanic's experience, qualifications, training, and certification. Several club officials suggest looking for certification by the National Institute for Automotive Service Excellence (NIASE) and for diplomas from vocational diagnostic training programs.

Joseph P. Hill, diagnostic center coordinator for the southern California club, says that if a car owner feels the diagnostic findings are excessive, if the facility begins applying pressure to have the car fixed there, or uses scare tactics regarding the urgency of needed repairs, it's best to pay the fee and leave immediately. Go somewhere else, and get another opinion.

Hill also recommends having the diagnostic center list separately repairs that should be performed immediately for safety reasons, or to prevent breakdowns or costlier repairs later, and those that can wait. The most important systems to be considered from a safety standpoint are brakes, tires, steering, and suspension.

Independent diagnostic centers not connected with a repair facility:

Auto Analysts, Sacramento, California
Auto Analysts, Denver, Colorado
Bear Manufacturers, Rock Island, Illinois
Farrar Brown Car Check, Biddeford, Maine
Lowry Service Center, Minneapolis, Minnesota
Ray Otto, Lake City Mobil, Seattle, Washington (includes limited
auto repair for regular customers)
Riverside Auto Lab, Riverside, California
Somerset Auto Diagnosis, Somerville, New Jersey

Auto clubs offering independent diagnosis:

California State Auto Association Clubs
150 Van Ness Avenue
San Francisco, California 94102

St. Louis, Missouri, Auto Club
3917 Lindell Boulevard
St. Louis, Missouri 63108

San Jose Auto Club
Cardoc Diagnosis Center
La Mesa, California 92041

In Summary

Where you take your car for service or repair is ultimately your decision. There is no "right" or even "best" place. Each type of facility must be judged on its individual merits, the service repairs necessary, and the choice available in the area. Our purpose here is to acquaint you with the various types of facilities usually available so that you can better judge how they fit your particular needs.

Always keep in mind that cars are complicated and that a good mechanic is not some uneducated lackey but, rather, a highly skilled technician whose services are in demand and whose judgment and counsel should always be considered. Our best advice is that you find a good mechanic or repair shop *before* you actually need to have your car fixed. Pay a visit, and say you're looking for a regular and dependable place to do business. Take your car in for a checkup and some relatively minor (and inexpensive) repairs or service the first time. Don't be the least bit reluctant or shy about letting the owner know you are checking him out. The fact that you are a selective and demanding consumer is complimentary to the people you choose to do business with, and they will often work a little harder than usual to please you.

Chapter 6

The Anatomy of an Automobile

Let's face it, modern automobiles are complex machines, and the technical manuals describing how they work weren't written for the average person. In this chapter and the next we explain how your car operates and what sometimes goes wrong with it. You'll also find your own troubleshooting guide to help you recognize what may be wrong the next time your car is acting up, won't start, or simply "doesn't sound right." In addition, we offer some practical suggestions to help you explain what's wrong with your car when you have to take it in for repairs.

It isn't necessary for you to be a mechanic in order to understand the basics of what makes your car go. A little knowledge can often protect you from unscrupulous repairmen who might try to feed you some mumbo jumbo. If you are told that your car's "flagillator isn't spinning as it should when the jiggerwhatzit commensurates with the elongated zippophonic doozits," you can just smile and say, "Bullfeathers, Buddy."

After all, as my wife aptly put it, "It's pretty darned difficult to take good care of something when you don't understand how it works in the first place." We think this chapter and the next will fix that.

The Major Systems

A car is generally divided into two major parts, the *body* and the *chassis.* The body is made up of a shell of sheet metal, with doors and

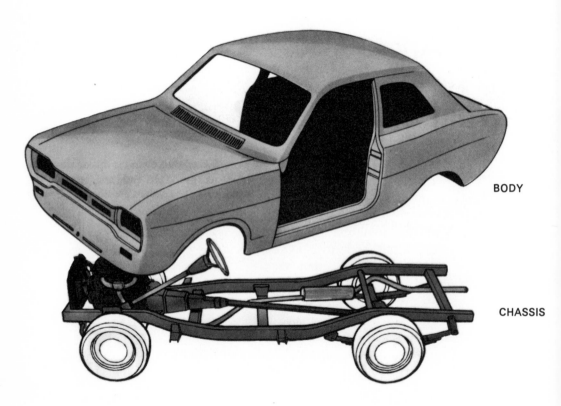

BODY

CHASSIS

The two main parts of a car are called the body and the chassis.

windows. The front (unless you have a rear-engine car) protects the engine, the middle carries people, and the rear holds luggage and probably a spare tire. Inside, the body is designed to protect you, to keep you as comfortable as possible, and to give you maximum control when you're driving. Built into the car's body is insulating material which protects you from outside heat, cold, and noise. If it weren't for this, it would be so noisy driving along at highway speeds you would have to shout to be heard by someone sitting right next to you. The insulation is placed along the floor and roof, and in the partitions separating you from the engine and the trunk.

If you unfasten all the bolts and connections and lift the body off, what remains underneath is the chassis. The chassis consists of several different systems and devices, all of which we'll describe in more detail later. Right now, however, let's take a quick look at the major chassis components.

The *frame* is a rugged structure built in the shape of a ladder or sometimes a giant X; it is made of heavy steel and reinforced with crosspieces. This is the foundation for the car body. The body and frame are joined together with fasteners. Rubber insulation blocks are usually placed where the body and chassis join in order to reduce noise and vibration. Bolted onto the front and rear of the frame are the bumpers. Sometimes the frame is built into the body, in which case, it's called an integral frame. When auto makers talk about "unitized" construction, they're referring to this kind of frame.

Fastened onto the front of the frame over the front axle is the *engine*. As in the body, insulation is used to prevent noise and vibration from traveling along the frame and getting inside the car. Behind the engine comes the *power train*, also supported in position by the frame. The power train includes the *transmission,* the *drive line, differential,* and the *rear axle*. The power train simply transmits the power generated by the engine to the rear wheels and makes them turn either forward or backward.

To save you and your car from being jarred to pieces, a method of springing is used between the wheels and the frame. This is called the *suspension* system. A combination of springs and shock absorbers works together to give you a smooth ride. You control the car through a *steering* system connected to the front wheels. This system includes the steering wheel and column, the steering gear, and a set of linkages. Among the most important parts of any car are the brakes. All we need to say about them now is that each wheel has one.

These—with only minor variations—are the major components or systems of all cars. Now we'll go into more detail, explaining exactly what happens from the moment you turn the key and drive away from the curb until the car is shut down again.

The Power Plant

Everyone knows that gasoline will burn. But if it is sprayed into a container with the lid on and then ignited, the mixture of gasoline and air will explode and blow the lid off with a tremendous force. What happens is this. Gasoline burns much quicker in its vapor form than in its liquid form; and its rapid expansion from heat causes it to take up more space, resulting in what we call an explosion. Remember this basic law of physics and you have the principle of the internal combustion engine, which simply means that the engine produces power by burning fuel within its own confines.

The task of the engine is to control that power capable of blowing the lid off and convert it into mechanical energy capable of moving the car. Imagine the same container or canister turned upside down with two holes drilled in the closed end and two valves fitted into each of the holes. One valve will open to allow the air/fuel mixture into the container and be called the *intake* valve. The other will open to release chemicals that were not burned and will be called, appropriately, the *exhaust* valve. A third hole is then drilled in the closed end, and a spark plug, which will provide an electric spark to ignite the fuel, is inserted.

A second cylinder, also open at one end, but slightly smaller in circumference and only about half the length of the larger container, will be necessary to build our imaginery engine. This second cylinder will be called a *piston*. Next we'll fasten a metal rod to the inside of our second cylinder, or piston, and call it a *connecting rod*. The upper end of the connecting rod is secured to the piston by what is called a *piston pin*. The piston is now inserted inside the first cylinder through the open end. It must fit snugly but still be able to move up and down freely inside the cylinder. The lower end of the connecting rod is now joined to a *crankshaft* by means of a bearing. A crankshaft is a strong metal shaft with cranks for each cylinder that convert the up-and-down motion of the piston and connecting rod into a revolving motion. It's similar to the way the up-and-down motion of your legs while pedaling a bicycle is converted into the circular motion of the chain sprocket. At one end of the crankshaft we attach a heavy, flat disk called a *flywheel*. The flywheel converts the rather jerky movement of the crankshaft into a smooth, spinning motion.

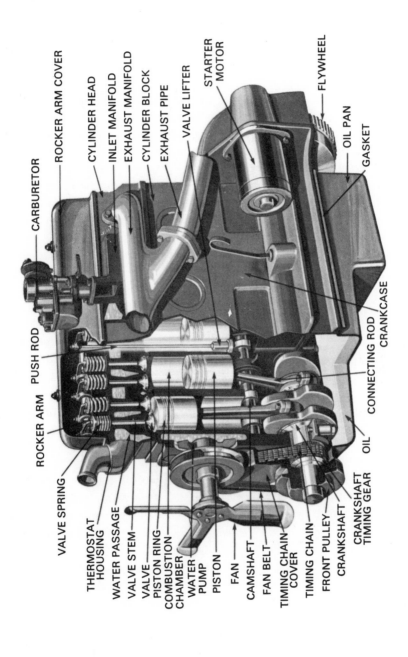

CARBURETOR

ROCKER ARM COVER

CYLINDER HEAD

INLET MANIFOLD

EXHAUST MANIFOLD

CYLINDER BLOCK

EXHAUST PIPE

VALVE LIFTER

STARTER MOTOR

FLYWHEEL

OIL PAN

GASKET

CRANKCASE

CONNECTING ROD

OIL

CRANKSHAFT TIMING GEAR

CRANKSHAFT

FRONT PULLEY

TIMING CHAIN

TIMING CHAIN COVER

FAN BELT

CAMSHAFT

FAN

PISTON

WATER PUMP

COMBUSTION CHAMBER

PISTON RING

VALVE

VALVE STEM

WATER PASSAGE

THERMOSTAT HOUSING

VALVE SPRING

ROCKER ARM

PUSH ROD

Cutaway illustration showing the various components of an engine.

Now that we have some of the basic elements of the engine assembled, we'll describe what actually happens when you start your car.

Unless your car is powered by a rotary engine, it is what's commonly known as a *four-cycle* power plant. You'll see what this means when we fire up our model.

Stroke 1: Intake. The piston is in the upper part of the cylinder; the intake valve is open and the exhaust valve is closed. Now we spin the flywheel and crankshaft; this moves the piston down inside the cylinder. At the same time, we spray the air and gasoline mixture into the cylinder through the intake valve.

Stroke 2: Compression. At the bottom of the first stroke the crankshaft has made half a turn. At the beginning of the second stroke it will continue turning and begin to push the rod and piston upward in the cylinder. Since the intake valve is now closed, the air/fuel mixture has no way out and is compressed at the top of the cylinder as the piston moves up. The crankshaft has now made one complete turn or revolution.

Stroke 3: Power. The piston is now at the top of its stroke, the mixture is completely compressed, and both valves remain closed. Now we activate the spark plug, which ignites the fuel mixture. (We'll explain a little later on how the electrical system works.) The rapidly expanding gases from the fire within the cylinder forces the piston down. The connecting rod, moving down with the piston, pushes hard on the crankshaft and the flywheel moves faster. The engine is now under its own power, and the crankshaft has now made one and a half turns.

Stroke 4: Exhaust. Our piston is now at the bottom of the stroke, and the crankshaft, now under engine power, pushes the piston upward. The intake valve remains closed, but as the piston travels back up toward the top of the cylinder the exhaust valve opens allowing the burned gases to escape. At this point the crankshaft has made two complete turns.

Our engine has now completed the four strokes—intake, compression, power, exhaust—which produce enough power to move the automobile. Keep in mind that in each four-stroke cycle the crankshaft makes two complete turns, or half a revolution for each stroke of the piston. And, although there are four strokes to each cycle, only one of these strokes delivers power to the crankshaft.

The piston doesn't stop after one cycle, of course. As soon as it reaches the top of the exhaust stroke, it starts down again on the intake

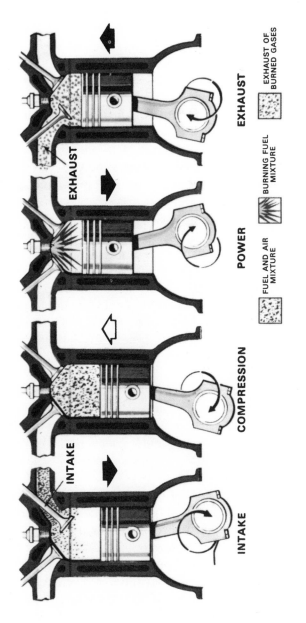

The four strokes of a four-cycle engine.

stroke of another complete cycle and keeps repeating these up-and-down cycles as long as the engine is running, several hundred to even many thousand times a minute.

We have been discussing the combustion cycle of only one cylinder, but car engines usually have four, six, or eight cylinders. Regardless of how many cylinders your car has, however, each of them operates in the same way, but at slightly different time intervals. Since each cylinder must withstand the tremendous heat and violent shock from the continuous and rapid up-and-down motions of the piston, they are cast from strong metal to form what is called the cylinder or engine *block*. The number of cylinders and the manner in which they are arranged determines the style of engine. Here are descriptions of the major engine arrangements used in most cars today:

In-line. The cylinders—either four or six (although sometimes eight)—are formed alongside each other in a row.

V-type. Sometimes this formation has six or twelve cylinders, but the most common variety is with eight—hence, V8. Cylinders are arranged in two equal rows, usually forming an angle of 90 degrees. The crankshaft is at the bottom of the V. The V-shaped engine is considered durable because it is compact and fairly low; the crankshaft is short and therefore stronger than in some other engine configurations.

Horizontal opposed. In this formation, four or six cylinders are arranged horizontally in two banks with the crankshaft between them. It's as if a V-shaped engine had been pressed flat.

Now let's look at the basic structure of the engine, using the in-line six as a model. Below the cylinder block is the *crankcase* which houses the crankshaft. Each of the six pistons is attached to the crankshaft by a connecting rod. On top of the cylinder block is the *cylinder head,* which forms the top part of the *combustion chamber* where the fuel mixture burns.

The crankshaft is the backbone of the engine. In the in-line six there are not one but six cylinders and pistons, each with its separate connecting rod joined to an individual crank on the crankshaft. The crankshaft itself is suspended in the crankcase by bearings which permit it to rotate several thousand times each minute without coming loose. That's why it's considered the backbone of the engine.

Each piston must suck in the mixture on the intake stroke, squeeze it on compression, take the full impact on the power stroke, and push out the burned gases on the exhaust stroke. Since this rugged job is performed several hundred to several thousand times a minute precision machining is a must. On the upper side of the cylinder head are the *rocker arms,* mechanisms that work the valves for the pistons. The rocker arms are protected by a cover that fits over the cylinder head and is called, appropriately, a rocker-arm cover. Bolted onto the bottom of the engine is the oil pan, which forms the crankcase and holds the engine oil that circulates through the power plant to lubricate many of the moving parts. All of these metal parts are supposed to fit together and form airtight or oiltight seals. With just metal to metal a seal would be impossible, so *gaskets* made of fibrous material are fitted between metal parts: the cylinder head and engine block, the crankcase and oil pan. If you spot any oil drippings under your car, chances are they are due to a leaky gasket.

Gaskets aren't always suitable, however. To create an airtight seal between the piston and the cylinder wall, a number of expanding rings, called *piston rings,* are fitted into grooves around the piston. These rings press out against the cylinder wall and provide a seal. Since the temperature inside the combustion chambers often reaches 2000 degrees Fahrenheit, it is obviously impossible to use anything other than specially heat-treated metal for sealing. Anything else would burn up in seconds.

Although we'll get into the importance of lubrication a little later, it's important right now to mention another function of the piston rings. Oil is splashed onto the cylinder walls from the crankcase as the engine runs in order to reduce friction and the resulting wear. The piston rings, as part of their sealing job, also sweep this oil down the cylinder walls on the down stroke to prevent it from getting into the combustion chamber.

As we mentioned earlier, the cylinders do not fire simultaneously (although the firing order takes place in such rapid succession it would be all but impossible for the human eye to perceive any sequence). Nor do they fire in chronological order, but, rather, in alternating fashion: 1-5-3-6-2-4. The firing order is carefully calculated to balance the strain on the crankshaft and provide a smoother-running engine. If the firing order were numerical in sequence it would set up a tremendous vibration that would impose a stress on the crankshaft and even the motor mounts that hold the engine in place on the frame. In other words, the irregular firing order is employed to create a kind of balance or rhythm.

Each cylinder has two valves, as you now know, which means our six-cylinder model has twelve—each of which must open and close at precisely the right instant. This job is performed through the aid of the *camshaft.* If the crankshaft is the backbone of the engine, then the camshaft must be considered the stomach, for it is the carefully machined shaft that metabolizes the energy the engine produces as it runs. The camshaft is a durable shaft of metal with a series of elliptical lobes of hardened metal machined onto it. These lobes are called cams, and there is one for every valve. The camshaft is positioned parallel to the crankshaft and, in the case of our six-cylinder engine, above it in the crankcase. The crankshaft drives the camshaft by means of *timing gears* (which may or may not use a timing chain). These gears are arranged so that the camshaft rotates at only half the speed of the crankshaft, and they are a vital link in getting the valves to open and close at precisely the right moment. The cams or lobes are what actually initiate the opening of the valves. As the high part of the elliptical lobe rotates, it triggers the *hydraulic valve lifter* (or *mechanical tappets* in some cars) by a long *push rod* that moves up and down, working the rocker arm that in turn pushes down on the valve stem, causing the valve to open. After the lobe passes the high part of its elliptical shape, the *valve spring* closes the valve. Each of the cam lobes has a different position on the shaft, with every one timed to open or close its valve at a precise instant. You may have heard of *overhead cam* engines or *dual overhead cam* engines. In these more sophisticated power plants the camshaft is located above the cylinders thus eliminating the need for push rods. This makes for a stronger engine capable of turning at higher revolutions per minute and producing greater power for its size.

One revolution of the crankshaft is what car buffs and mechanics are referring to when they talk about revolutions per minute or rpm. The *tachometer* in your car (if it is so equipped) registers these revolutions. For example, if you are driving down the highway and the tachometer indicates 3500 rpm, it means the crankshaft is completing that many revolutions each minute. The tachometer usually takes its reading electronically from the ignition.

Delivering the Fuel

Gasoline is stored in the *fuel tank,* which is usually located in the rear of most cars, as far away from the passengers as possible for safety reasons. This tank contains baffles to prevent the fuel from sloshing around. It also has a level indicator which is connected electrically to a gauge on the instrument panel. The tank is connected by a *fuel line* to the *fuel pump.* Before entering the fuel line, the gasoline passes through

The fuel tank on most cars is located at the rear, underneath the car.

This inexpensive fuel filter should be replaced regularly.

The carburetor is an intricate device which should not be adjusted by amateurs.

a screen in the tank; this screen filters out sediment that may have settled in the bottom of the tank.

The fuel pump, which is attached to the side of the engine, pumps the gasoline from the tank through the fuel line to the carburetor. This pump is usually operated mechanically from the camshaft, but in some cars it is driven electrically. In the mechanical variety, a lobe on the camshaft moves a rocker arm up and down. This rocker arm is fastened to a rod which in turn is connected to a diaphragm inside the pump. The up-and-down motion of the diaphragm pumps the gasoline from the tank, along the fuel line, through the pump and along more fuel line again to the *carburetor.*

Before entering the carburetor, the gasoline passes through a second filter located either between the fuel pump and the carburetor or in the carburetor itself. This filter is often the source of trouble for car owners because they don't have it checked and cleaned regularly. Consequently, tiny particles of dirt build up, and the flow of fuel into the carburetor is reduced, resulting in loss of power. This filter should be removed and cleaned or replaced at least once a year (preferably every six months or 6000 miles).

The carburetor itself is an intricate and sensitive device that is surprisingly simple in concept. It used to be called a "mixing valve," which is still a pretty accurate description, since its function is to receive the gasoline and mix it in the right proportions with air and then feed the mixture into the combustion chambers. To explain how that works, we'll describe a simplified version. We start with a vertical hollow tube called an *air horn,* which leads into the *intake manifold.* This manifold leads directly to the cylinders. On the intake stroke there is a partial vacuum in each cylinder. This creates a strong current of air that moves down the air horn.

On the outside of the air horn is a *float bowl.* This bowl is where the gasoline arrives on its trip from the fuel pump. A needle valve connected to a float keeps the gasoline in the bowl at a constant level, the same way the float works in your toilet bowl, preventing water from flooding the bathroom. Tiny particles of dust often lodge between this needle and its seat in the valve, thus preventing the float bowl from performing its job. This can usually be prevented by making sure the fuel filter is clean.

Inside the air horn another piece of tubing is fitted, shaped like an hourglass, which narrows the passageway of the horn. This tubing is called a *venturi.* Its function is to increase the speed of the air current through itself. A small tube called the *main discharge nozzle* connects the float bowl to the venturi. When the engine is running, the strong current of air rushing down the venturi sucks out gasoline from the discharge nozzle in the form of a spray. This mixture of air and gasoline passes through the intake manifold and into the combustion chamber through smooth channels called *ports*.

We must have a way of regulating the flow of fuel mixture into the cylinders or else the engine would be running full blast all the time. This is accomplished by fitting a metal disk called a *throttle valve*, or *butterfly*, below the venturi. The throttle is hinged on a shaft and is connected by a linkage to the accelerator pedal inside the car. The more you push the pedal with your foot, the wider the throttle opens, the more mixture is sucked into the combustion chambers, and the faster the car goes.

The carburetor has still another control valve, which you usually use in the mornings or when your car has been sitting for some time and the engine is cold. It's called a *choke*. The choke is just like the regular throttle, but it's fitted higher up in the air horn to partially close off the air passage and create a richer mixture of fuel (less air and more fuel). On most domestic cars today, the choke is operated automatically by a thermostat.

As you might imagine, it's just as important for the air that is drawn into the carburetor, and ultimately into the cylinders, to be free of dust as it is for the gasoline. To accomplish this, carburetors are fitted with an *air cleaner*. This is a big circular device on top of the engine. You can quickly and easily spot it when you lift up the hood. It cleans the air by trapping dust in a specially treated paper filter, which is another item that should be checked regularly by either you or your mechanic.

So far we've traced the flow of gasoline from the fuel tank through the fuel line, the pump, the filter, the carburetor, the intake manifold, and into the combustion chamber. But what happens to the burned gases and other wastes that are evacuated from the combustion chambers on the exhaust stroke? These are routed through the *exhaust manifold*, the *exhaust pipe*, the *muffler* (a metal box packed with sound-deadening materials to reduce noise from the engine), and out through the tail pipe. Some cars are equipped with a dual system that adds to performance by providing better release of these gases and reducing back pressure that would otherwise build up in the combustion chambers.

One of the major reasons why mufflers wear out is that for every gallon of gasoline burned, roughly about the same amount of water vapor (which comes from both the air and gasoline) is formed within

The air cleaner sits on top of the engine, covering up much of it. When the filter inside the air cleaner becomes clogged with dirt, it must be cleaned or replaced.

the exhaust system. When cars are driven short distances (generally under 15 miles) the exhaust system does not heat up enough to evacuate this water and dry out the muffler and tail pipe. The water then condenses and mixes with acids also formed by combustion; the result is corrosion and rust.

There is one more important item we must mention before moving on to the other systems that work to make your car go. Exhaust gases contain carbon monoxide. It can cause headaches or drowsiness, and in sufficient amounts, it is deadly. That's why it's important for you to keep tabs on your exhaust system. If you suspect a leak, keep the windows open and take your car to be checked immediately. If your suspicions are confirmed, have it fixed on the spot.

Keeping It Cool

The temperature in the combustion chambers of an engine reaches about 2000 degrees Fahrenheit. Since the melting point of iron is only slightly higher than that, it's necessary to cool the engine as it's operating. The cooling system in modern cars is based on the idea that the best way to cool something down is either to pour water on it or blow on it.

Before describing the system, which is actually quite simple, we should point out that it serves more than one function. It removes excessive heat, keeps the engine at an even operating temperature, and allows the engine to reach that temperature quickly. In addition, it supplies heat to keep the driver and passengers warm when necessary.

Here's how it works. Since all the heat is generated in the cylinder block and the cylinder head, these sections are built with hollow walls and passages called *water jackets*. At the front of the engine is a *water pump*, which is driven off the crankshaft. Its job is to circulate the water. In front of the water pump is a fan, which in most cars is mounted on a shaft extending through the water pump. Both fan and pump are driven by a *fan belt* connected to a pulley mounted in front of the crankshaft. As the crankshaft turns the belt rotates the water pump and fan. Since the entire cooling system is dependent upon this rubber belt, it must be kept in good condition and be properly adjusted.

Since even circulating water will heat up eventually, a *radiator* is used to cool it down. Water circulates out of the engine through rubber hoses into the top of the radiator where it travels down through a series of small tubes called the *core* and back out the bottom and through the engine again. These tubes have air spaces between them and are finned

Exhaust pipes and mufflers should be checked for holes and leaks. Exhaust gases that escape into the car are dangerous.

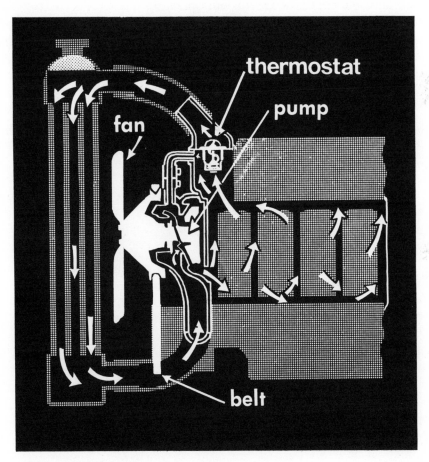

Illustration of a typical cooling system.

to permit the water to be cooled by the air rushing in from the grill in the front of the car. This cooling action is speeded up by the fan, which helps draw the air through the radiator.

A thermostat controls the system, just as a thermostat controls the heating system in many homes today. By regulating the amount of water flow it permits the engine to warm up quickly, and it also maintains the engine at an efficient operating temperature in any kind of weather. When the engine is cold, such as when you first start your car in the morning or during extremely cold winter weather, this thermostat shuts off the flow of coolant through the radiator altogether.

Sometimes when your car engine is idling in heavy traffic on a hot day, the radiator may not be able to handle the job of keeping it cool. You can often prevent overheating, however, by moderately accelerating the engine in neutral; this increases the speed of the fan and water pump, draws cool air in through the radiator faster, and speeds up the flow of coolant.

The hot water in the cooling system also supplies heat for the passenger compartment by circulating through a heater built like a miniature radiator. A fan in the heater drives the warm air into the passenger compartment and to the defrosters which throw a blast of warm air onto the windshield.

Water makes a fine cooling agent for engines except for three inherent weaknesses: it freezes, it boils at a relatively low temperature, and it permits rust and corrosion. For these reasons it is wise to mix an *antifreeze coolant* with the water. This coolant contains ethylene glycol and chemicals that inhibit rusting and corrosion. The mixture generally should be about 50-50, although in colder climates it's a good idea to increase the ratio of antifreeze. Coolant also offers better protection in hot weather since it has a much higher boiling point than water.

Because of a certain amount of leakage and natural evaporation it's necessary to check the coolant or water level in your car's radiator regularly. Be sure, however, to do this only when the engine is cold, or you could be badly burned. Since the cooling system is pressurized to raise the boiling point, removing the cap when the engine is hot can send a spray of scalding water all over you and any bystanders. If your engine does heat up for any reason, either shut it down and open the hood to allow cool air to circulate better or pull into the first gas station and run water over the outside of the radiator for a few minutes with the engine running before gradually releasing the pressurized radiator cap and adding water.

So far we've talked about water as a cooling agent, but some engines are air-cooled. These power plants are usually made of aluminum, which is a good heat conductor, and designed with fins to direct cool air over the hottest parts. These engines require a powerful fan, driven by the engine, to drive away excess heat. Air-cooled engines warm up quickly, are simpler in design, and eliminate much of the maintenance required by a water-cooling system. Cooling by air, however, is most effective in smaller engines like the Volkswagen since an enormous fan would be necessary to do the job on the larger power plants of most American cars.

Reducing Wear

Since most of the internal moving parts of an automobile engine are metal rubbing against metal, it's necessary to reduce friction and the resulting wear with some form of lubrication. Motor oil lubricates, cleans, and helps to cool the engine; it also helps the piston rings provide an effective seal. To provide satisfactory cooling and lubrication, oil must flow freely over a wide range of temperatures. The consistency of oil, or its resistance to flow, is called *viscosity*. Car owners' manuals usually recommend the SAE (Society of Automotive Engineers) grade or grades to be used under certain conditions. For instance, SAE 10W might be recommended for winter use and SAE 30 for summer. Multigrade oils, such as SAE 10W-40, might also be recommended, particularly for year-round use.

While the engine is running, the oil is subjected to friction, heat, chemical changes, and contamination from impurities. This leads to eventual deterioration of the oil's protective qualities. For this reason it is essential to change the oil and the oil filter at regular intervals as recommended in the owner's manual.

Generating and Storing Electricity

Your car won't run without electricity, which is necessary for combustion. Since it obviously can't be plugged into a stationary outlet, it must supply all its own electrical needs. This is accomplished through a system which uses the car's mechanical energy to generate and store electricity. This *charging system*, as it is called, includes the *alternator* (*generator* on older cars), the *voltage regulator*, and the *battery*.

The alternator is attached to the front of the engine and is driven off the crankshaft, using the same belt that drives the water pump. The alternator converts the engine's mechanical energy into electrical energy.

Since the alternator is driven by the fan belt, the belt must be adjusted for the proper tension if the alternator is to work correctly.

Here are the pieces it takes to overhaul the ignition system completely. At the top are the points, condenser, rotor, distributor cap, and the coil; at the bottom is a set of spark plugs.

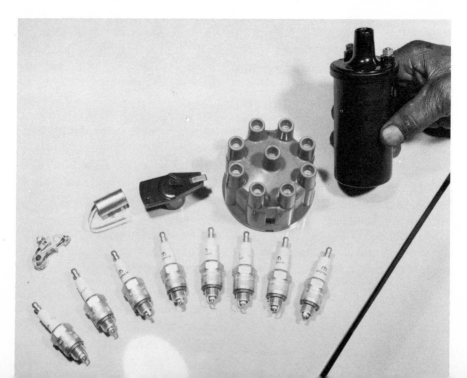

The alternator's output of electrical energy must be controlled or it will damage the electrical system by producing too much current. This is where the important voltage regulator comes into play. It controls or regulates the alternator's output. The third part of the charging system, the battery, uses chemical means to store electrical energy and to supply it for starting the car and operating electrical equipment when the engine is not running. The alternator supplies electricity to keep the battery charged; the voltage regulator controls the current to meet the battery's varying needs.

These three components work together to supply electricity for the *ignition system*, the *starter motor*, and other electrical equipment (radio, clock, power windows, lights, etc.).

Some sort of spark is necessary to trigger combustion. This is achieved through the ignition system, which must produce a powerful current to ignite the fuel mixture in each cylinder at exactly the precise instant. To do this, it has two circuits: a *primary* circuit and a *secondary* circuit. In the primary circuit, when the ignition switch is turned on, current flows from the 12-volt battery, through a *resistor*, which restricts voltage, to the *ignition coil*. The coil has two windings, a *primary winding* and a *secondary winding*. These windings step up the voltage from the 12-volt battery to a much higher voltage, so that a strong spark is delivered to each combustion chamber.

In order to produce a spark in each combustion chamber at the right moment, the circuit through the coil must be repeatedly stopped and started again. This is the job of the *breaker points*, which are located in the *distributor*. A shaft through the center of the distributor is driven from the camshaft. A cam on the distributor shaft opens and closes the breaker points, thus making and breaking the circuit in the coil. To prevent the current from jumping across the points as they are opening, a condenser is used to block the current.

A circuit is made up of a source of power (a battery), a conductor (a wire to carry the current), and one or more electrical devices operated by the current. An electrical circuit must be completed, or closed, in order to work. Since electricity can travel quite easily along the metal structure of a car, less wiring is necessary. The *negative terminal* of the battery is connected or *grounded* to the steel frame of the car or to the engine block. The *positive terminal* connects to the starter motor, and is also connected to the distributor. This little device, which is not much larger than a fist, has the big job of feeding the current to the spark plugs at exactly the right moment. Although your car's battery produces only 12 volts, each time the breaker points in the distributor open, the secondary winding in the coil produces 20,000 volts or more. That's a current with a kick.

Current from the 12-volt battery flows through the resistor, through the primary winding of the coil, through the closed breaker points, through the ground, and back to the battery. When the points open, the primary circuit travels through the condenser to the ground. In the secondary circuit the voltage goes from the secondary winding of the coil, along a wire, and down through the middle of the distributor cap, where it makes contact with a *rotor* inside the cap. This rotor is on top of the distributor shaft and spins around inside the cap. Arranged around the inside of this cap are metal terminals, one for each cylinder in the engine. Connected to each terminal is a separate wire leading from the distributor cap to a spark plug, which is screwed into the top of each cylinder.

As the outer end of the rotor passes beneath each terminal it transmits the current—20,000 volts or more—which travels up through the cap, along the wire to the spark plug, and down the *central electrode*. A small gap separates this central electrode of the spark plug from the *side electrode* in the plug, which is grounded to the engine. When the current arrives at the gap between the two electrodes it has to jump across. In so doing, it creates a spark that ignites the fuel in the cylinders.

In order to start the engine, however, we need a device to spin the flywheel so the crankshaft will turn and move the pistons up and down, just as we did by hand in our imaginary one-cylinder engine. This is performed by the starter motor; its job is exactly the opposite of that of the alternator. While the alternator turns the engine's mechanical energy into electrical energy, the starter motor converts electrical energy into mechanical energy through a spinning motion.

The starter motor is located near the flywheel, at the lower rear of most engines. A ring gear is fastened on the rim of the flywheel, and on the shaft of the starter there's another much smaller gear or *pinion* that can mesh with the teeth of the ring gear. When you turn the ignition key to the start position, the *solenoid* switch sends current to the starter, pushing the pinion forward on the shaft until it meshes with the ring gear on the flywheel. As the flywheel picks up speed, the pinion gear is forced out of its mesh with the ring gear on the flywheel. This is necessary to protect the starter motor or it would continue turning and quickly overheat.

At the same moment that the starter motor spins the flywheel, current is sent out from the battery, is multiplied by the coil, and then

The starter motor engages the ring gear, which fits around the edge of the flywheel, and spins the flywheel to start the engine.

routed by the distributor in correct doses to the spark plugs. In an instant the engine roars to life. But you won't be going anywhere unless you have some method of getting all that power to the wheels.

Putting That Power to Work

The job of the *power train* is to deliver engine power to the rear wheels. But it's not enough merely to deliver that power; the power train also has to control it so that the car can accelerate gradually, come to a stop, go forward or backward, vary its speed, and turn corners. This is accomplished through a system of gears that are as important as they are complex. The three main components of this system are the *transmission, drive line*, and *rear axle*, which also includes the *differential*.

There are two basic types of transmissions: *standard* and *automatic*. Standard transmissions require manual shifting and use of a foot pedal called a *clutch*. Since standard transmissions are simpler in construction, we'll explore them first.

As soon as the engine starts, the flywheel begins to spin. The problem is to connect the spinning flywheel smoothly with the power train and then to disconnect it while the engine is still running. This is the job of the clutch, which relies on the power of friction to do its work.

Let's imagine two disks on separate shafts facing each other, with only one disk turning. As soon as the two disks are pressed firmly together, the turning disk will transmit its motion to the other and both will turn together as one unit. It's on this simple principle that the clutch operates. A clutch plate, faced on both sides with friction material, is connected to the transmission shaft. A pressure plate forces this clutch plate against the turning flywheel, which turns the clutch plate and the transmission shaft. This action is controlled by the driver through the clutch pedal, which permits application of the clutch gradually so that the flywheel's motion passes smoothly to the transmission shaft.

The transmission delivers power from the flywheel to the drive line, and it also controls the ratio between the engine's speed in rpm and the speed of the drive wheels. It becomes necessary to change the speed ratio between the engine and the wheels as the car accelerates or you wouldn't be able to travel very fast. This is where *torque* comes into play. Torque is a twisting or turning motion. For example, you produce or use torque when you insert a screw into wood. A large amount of torque is required when your car has to accelerate from a dead stop or climb a steep hill. The standard transmission provides the necessary torque and varies the rpm ratio through the use of gears. When the transmission increases torque it decreases speed and vice versa.

Gears are basically toothed wheels. The transmission, or gearbox, as it is frequently called, consists of several sets of different-sized gears in constant mesh. Mechanical locking devices on the gears enable selection of the desired set. The transmission also contains a gear set which reverses the direction of rotation of the drive line. This permits the car to be driven backward. Gear ratio is determined by the number of teeth on the gears. If the driving gear, for example, is smaller and has 20 teeth and the gear being driven is larger and has 40 teeth, the gear ratio is two to one. In this manner the transmission is actually able to multiply torque.

The driver changes gears by moving the *gearshift lever* on the steering column or the floor. Most standard transmissions offer three forward speeds and one for reverse. The four- and five-speed transmission with the shifting lever usually on the floor, has grown increasingly popular in recent years, but regardless of the number of forward gears, all standard transmissions operate basically in the same way.

When the driver first starts out, he uses the lowest gear, which provides maximum torque at low speed; then he shifts to second and on to higher gears as the car's speed increases and torque is needed less. High-gear ratio is usually one to one, which means that both the driving gear and the one being driven are identical in size and number of teeth.

The job of the automatic transmission is the same, of course, but its methods are slightly different. In the standard transmission, two techniques are employed to transmit the flywheel's rotary motion (power) to the drive line: friction and gears. In the automatic transmission a third method is used: fluid. Instead of a clutch, automatic transmissions employ what is called the *fluid coupling*.

To visualize how the fluid coupling works, picture a circular jelly mould, shaped like half a hollow doughnut, with little walls or partitions called *vanes* fitted around the inside, similar to an ice tray. This device is called a *torus*. Next, we must fit a shaft into the center hole and then fill the torus with oil and spin the shaft. What happens? Just as you expected, centrifugal force throws oil out over the rim. We obviously need more parts if this torus is going to be of much help in transmitting torque. So we fill it with more oil. Then we mount a second torus upside down directly over—but not quite touching—the one filled with oil. Now we spin the lower torus. Once again the oil goes around in a rotary motion, and at the same time centrifugal force drives the oil up and over the rim. But this time the oil doesn't fly out. Instead, it flies up into the vanes of the upper torus and is then deflected back down into the lower one. This continuous round-and-round movement between the upper and lower torus is called the *vortex flow*. This is what happens. The oil flowing from the lower torus to the upper one is transmitting the motion of the lower one and causing the upper one to spin in the same direction.

In the actual situation in a car, the first torus is attached to the flywheel in a vertical position and is called the driving torus, or *pump*. The second torus, also vertical and not quite touching the first, is called the driven torus, or *turbine*. This one is connected to the transmission shaft. Both the pump and turbine are enclosed in an oil-filled casing.

When the flywheel begins turning, the oil starts rotating with the pump, but also moving in a vortex motion between the vanes of the pump and turbine. The vortex effect of the oil transmits the turning motion from the pump to the turbine, which also starts turning, until it reaches nearly the same speed. Likewise, as the flywheel and pump lose speed, the turbine and the transmission shaft slow down. Thus the fluid coupling produces the same results as the friction clutch, only smoother and without any help from the driver.

Although the automatic transmission eliminates much of the driver's work, you still have your part to play. You must select the gearing or range of speed ("drive," "low," or "reverse") through the use of a lever mounted on either the steering column or the floor. When you depress the accelerator you not only regulate the carburetor, but through

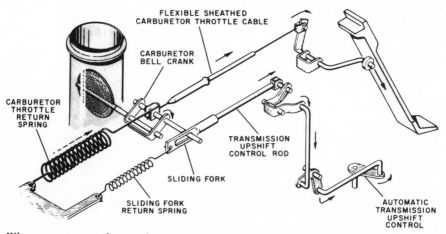

When you step on the accelerator you not only actuate the carburetor linkage, but the automatic transmission linkage as well.

The flat, squarish pan under the automatic transmission should be checked for leaks.

The propeller shaft (the pipe-like object on the left) is connected to the differential by means of a universal joint (seen in the center).

another set of linkages you also regulate the transmission's hydraulic system. Both standard and automatic transmissions are infinitely more complex than we've indicated here, but a basic understanding of the automobile is what we're striving for, not advanced technical knowledge. There are many books and manuals available if you need or want more detailed explanations.

The most important thing for you to remember about your car's transmission is that it requires constant lubrication and must be checked as regularly as the engine.

Now that we've gotten the engine running and the transmission shaft rotating, let's follow the rotary motion back through the drive line to the differential which rests in the middle of the rear axle, and then along the two side axles to the rear wheels.

The propeller shaft transmits the rotary motion from the transmission shaft to the differential. It is hollow, allowing it to withstand the twisting stress better than a solid piece would. It connects the transmission, which is fixed rigidly to the engine and frame, with the rear axle, which is connected to the frame by springs, and it moves up and down as the car travels along over uneven surfaces. Because of these movements, the propeller shaft cannot be fixed rigidly between the transmission and the differential. Instead, two *universal joints* (or "U-joints") are used as connections between the transmission and the differential. These joints are flexible, allowing rotary motion to pass from one shaft to another. A telescopic joint in the propeller shaft also permits a slight change in the length of the drive line, necessary when the car hits bumps.

The rear axle bears a large part of the car's weight and holds the rear wheels. It delivers torque from the propeller shaft to the rear wheels by means of a differential. This device not only transmits torque from the propeller shaft to the rear wheels, but also increases torque by reducing speed. The differential also allows each wheel to rotate at a different speed, which is necessary since the outer wheel travels farther than the inner wheel when the car is turning a corner. This means it must rotate faster.

Like the transmission and engine, the differential gears must be well lubricated. To make sure they're receiving that important protection, the oil level should be checked each time your car is in for service.

Smoothing the Ride

Without the *suspension system*, driving or riding in a car would be a

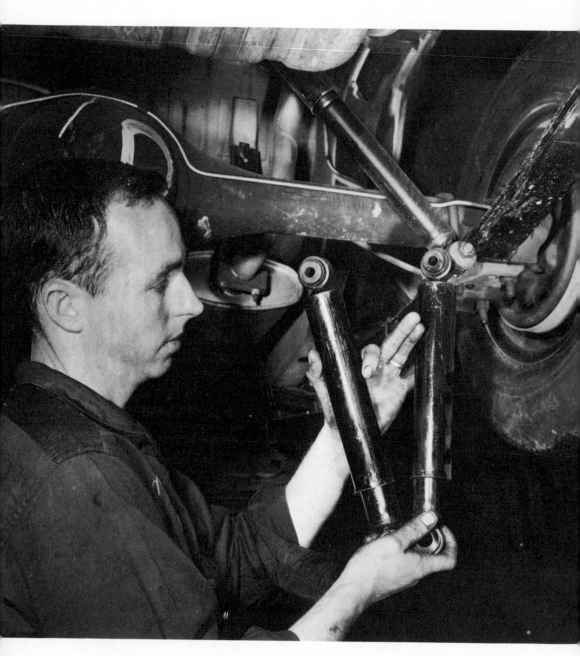

Shock absorbers control the up and down movement of the car as it goes over bumps in the road.

nerve-shattering experience. The driver and his passengers would be so badly jolted—almost continuously—that a ride of only a few miles could be tolerated. In addition, the car itself would soon fall apart from the continuous pounding. So it's necessary to have some effective way of cushioning the ride, yet making the car stable and safe to control. To do this, the frame is connected to the wheels or axles by *springs*, which, along with *shock absorbers*, are used for that necessary cushioning. Together the springs and shock absorbers comprise the suspension system. It could just as easily have been called the "cushioning system"; but technical types, like engineers and mechanics, don't think in the same terms as most of us. It's ironic, however, in this instance, because cushioning would be much more accurate both technically and descriptively.

At any rate, since the chassis and body of the car comprise more than 90 percent of a car's total weight, the suspension system allows the axles, wheels, and tires to bounce up and down as the car moves along, absorbing most of the violent bumps that would otherwise be transmitted through the car to the passengers.

Three kinds of springs are used: *coil, leaf,* and *torsion bar.* Coil springs are just what the name implies, coils of specially tempered steel. Leaf springs, used almost exclusively in rear-axle suspension, consist of leaves of flat steel, graduated in length, with the longest leaf on the top and the shortest on the bottom. The torsion bar, sometimes used instead of coil springs for front-wheel suspension, is a long bar of spring steel with one end clamped rigidly to the car frame and the other end left free to turn. When the free end turns, a twisting motion along the bar gives the same results as a spring.

If, however, a car were equipped only with springs it would bounce up and down dangerously each time it hit a bump in the road. To control this bouncing, oil-filled hydraulic shock absorbers are used in addition to the springs. They are made with two or more cylinders, one within the other, with a piston in the innermost cylinder. The upper part of the shock absorber is connected to the frame, and the lower part is connected to the axle. When the car passes over a bump, the hydraulic fluid is forced through small openings in the piston, absorbing the pounding and controlling the bouncing.

Springs rarely need replacing, but shock absorbers do wear out. If your car's shocks have more than 20,000 miles on them you should check to see if they're losing their cushioning power. To do this, simply press down on the fender above each wheel with all your weight and then release it. If the car returns to its normal posture immediately, the shocks are fine. But if it bounces two or three times before settling down, better start shopping for new shocks. If you're fairly certain that you'll be keeping your present car for at least another three or four years, it will probably be worth your while to invest in top-quality shocks, since these generally last twice and sometimes four or five times as long as the bargain variety. But even the cheapest shocks should give you about 15,000 miles of wear if most of your driving is on good roads.

Changing Direction

Now that we have an engine, a power train, and electrical and suspension systems, we need some way of controlling the car—something that will make it possible to guide the car down the road and around corners. That something, of course, is the steering system, which consists of a *steering wheel* and *shaft*, *steering gear*, *linkage*, *steering arms*, and *steering knuckles*.

When you turn the steering wheel, the shaft transmits the motion to the steering gear. As a safety feature in late-model cars, the shaft is designed to collapse several inches if the driver is thrown against it in a crash. The steering gear multiplies your turning effort in order to let you steer more easily. The steering gear also changes the rotary motion of the shaft into a lateral or side-to-side motion in the *pitman arm*, which is a lever extending from the steering gear. In power steering, hydraulic power is used to boost the turning force which the driver applies manually to the steering wheel. This power is supplied by a hydraulic *power steering pump* driven by a belt from the engine.

Each front wheel is supported on a steering knuckle that pivots on ball joints between an *upper* and a *lower control arm*. These control arms are pieces of steel attached horizontally at their inner ends to the frame. They pivot up and down, never sideways. The outer ends of the two arms are linked by a steering knuckle, which pivots between the arms on ball joints. Protruding from the knuckle is a spindle on which the wheel rotates.

The steering linkage, which is a series of rods, arms, and levers, is designed to transmit the movement of the pitman arm to the two steering arms, so that the two front wheels will turn in the same direction. This turning movement is controlled, however, so that when rounding a corner the inside wheel turns slightly more than the outside one, which must make a larger arc. The most common linkage arrangement includes a pitman arm, an *idler arm*, a *center link*, and two

The steering linkages should be checked regularly for wear and kept properly adjusted.

tie rods. The center link connects the pitman arm to the idler arm, which is secured to the frame. Each tie rod is fastened at one end to one of the steering arms, and at the other to the center link.

Now let's imagine you're turning a corner and see what happens. As you turn the steering wheel, the rotary motion is transmitted through the shaft into the steering gear, where it is converted into the side-to-side motion of the pitman arm. The pitman arm passes this motion on to the center link, which triggers the idler arm. The sole function of the idler arm is to help the center link move freely. As the center link moves, it pulls one tie rod and pushes the other, so that both wheels will pivot together to turn the car in the direction you want to go.

Steering systems in modern cars are rugged and strong. Chances are you'll never have trouble with any part of this system. But you should still have its components checked regularly for any signs of excessive wear, particularly the tie rods which take a tremendous beating even when you're cruising down a smooth expressway.

Slowing Down

We all know what brakes are for and how important they are to driving safety. But few drivers are aware of the simple applied physics involved in slowing and stopping a car. With rare exceptions, today all brake systems rely on *hydraulics*, which is a fancy word for the study of the pressure flow of liquids. Hydraulics and friction are the two scientific principles employed in modern braking systems. First, we'll look at hydraulics.

It's practically impossible to compress liquids, and they can transmit force and motion very effectively. When pressure is exerted on confined liquids, that pressure is transmitted—undiminished—in all directions, much in the same way as sound waves or water ripples fan out in all directions from their source.

Let's see how these principles are applied to help work the brakes on your car. The idea is to transmit the pressure from your foot when you depress the brake pedal inside the car to the brakes on each of the four wheels. The brake pedal is linked by a *push rod* to a *primary piston* in the *master cylinder*, which is attached to the engine side of the metal partition or firewall separating the passenger compartment from the engine. The primary piston then activates a *secondary piston.* One piston controls the rear brakes, the other the front ones. This is an obvious safety measure, since if one system fails you still have half your original stopping power, which is a hundred times better than none.

The master cylinder is connected to the brakes by means of *brake lines*. (Don't confuse these with the brake *linings*.) The brake lines are strong, lead-coated steel tubes built to withstand tremendous pressure. The entire system, including the master cylinder, is filled with a special hydraulic brake fluid.

As the driver depresses the brake pedal, the push rod transmits the thrust of the pedal to the two pistons in the master cylinder. The pistons then exert pressure on the fluid in the system. Since fluid can't be compressed, this pressure is transmitted through the brake lines to the brakes.

Most cars today are built with *drum* brakes on the rear wheels and *disc* brakes up front. To understand how the brakes on the wheels work, we must first distinguish between the parts that *rotate* and those which are *stationary* or fixed in position.

First let's discuss the fixed parts. We'll begin with the steering knuckle spindle, to which is bolted a circular *backing plate*. Two steel *brake shoes* are connected to the backing plate by an *anchor pin* near the top. Directly below the pin there's a *wheel cylinder* with a piston at each end. Each of these pistons presses against one of the brake shoes when activated. The bottom end of each shoe is attached to the adjuster screw, which lies horizontally or parallel to the ground. A heat-resistant brake lining, made of asbestos and other materials, is firmly secured to the outer surface of each brake shoe.

Now let's talk about the rotating parts. First, a *wheel hub* fits over and rotates around the spindle. The *brake drum*, which is attached to the hub, fits over the brake shoe assembly which *does not* rotate. The wheel then fits over the brake drum and is bolted to the hub, so that wheel, hub, and drum rotate as a single unit. This leaves the smoothly finished inner side of the brake drum spinning around the outside of the brake shoes.

When you step on the brake pedal, the hydraulic system is activated as described earlier. The two pistons inside the cylinder move outward, forcing the brake shoes out against the inner side of the brake drum, thus creating intense friction that slows or stops the rotating wheel. The brake linings and drum absorb the heat, which is carried away by circulating air currents.

Disc brakes also operate through hydraulics and friction, but with a quicker, smoother, and stronger gripping action. Let's see how this is done by returning to the steering knuckle, to which a *caliper* is bolted. To help you to understand what a caliper is and what it does, imagine

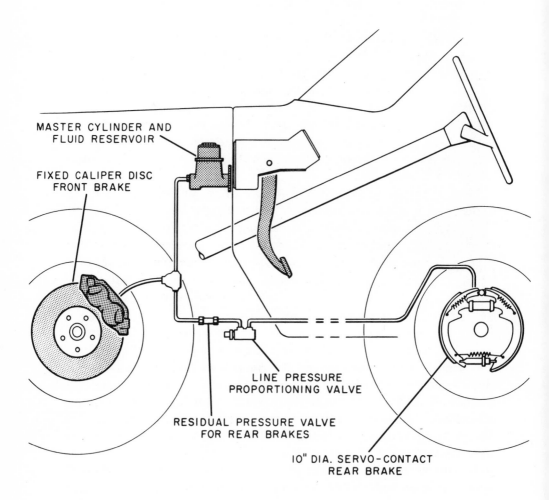

MASTER CYLINDER AND
FLUID RESERVOIR

FIXED CALIPER DISC
FRONT BRAKE

LINE PRESSURE
PROPORTIONING VALVE

RESIDUAL PRESSURE VALVE
FOR REAR BRAKES

10" DIA. SERVO-CONTACT
REAR BRAKE

Today most cars are built with a combination of disc brakes on the front wheels and drum brakes on the rear wheels.

The fluid level in the master cylinder should be checked regularly.

the wheel of an upended bicycle turning slowly. To stop the wheel, you grip it gently, but firmly, with your thumb and index finger—not enough to stop it abruptly, but rather to slow it gradually and smoothly. The caliper works in much the same way, only it performs the gripping action with two steel brake shoes, each fitted with an asbestos brake pad, that squeeze a spinning steel disc connected to the hub. The wheel is bolted to the hub; and the hub, disc, and wheel all rotate as one unit. When you step on the brake pedal, hydraulic pressure activates one or more pistons in the caliper, and the brake pads move together and clamp down on the disc.

Like drum brakes, the disc type are air cooled. But because the discs are exposed more to circulating air they cool much more quickly. Disc brakes are used on the front of many cars today since greater force or stopping power is required to slow the front wheels. A few high-performance production cars and just about all racing cars are equipped with disc brakes on all four wheels.

But whatever kind of brakes your car has, to derive the full benefits of the system, always make sure the hydraulic fluid level in the master cylinder is up to the full mark or within about a quarter of an inch of the top.

In Summary

This has been a very simplified description of how a car works. But learning is only a process of building, and you now have at least a good foundation. Try building on that foundation by inspecting your car yourself and getting acquainted with it. This effort is almost certain to pay off the next time something goes wrong.

Chapter 7

Getting Along with Your Car

If there's one thing everyone in the auto industry agrees on, it's the importance and value of regular care in preventing costly and inconvenient auto repairs. In fact, engineers and mechanics insist that regular service and attention will eliminate more than 70 percent of all auto repairs.

"It's amazing," mused one garage owner. "People invest thousands of dollars in a car and then don't bother with even the most basic maintenance. Maybe I'm something of a tightwad, but when I pay a lot of money for something—whatever it is—I intend to get my money's worth out of it."

As an example, this veteran auto repairman told of a young businessman who was furious when the engine froze up on his two-year-old Mustang. However, when told that his car had run dry of coolant, he merely shrugged indifferently. When questioned further, he admitted that he hadn't had the car serviced since the warranty expired—more than one year and nearly 15,000 miles earlier. "I just never seemed to have time. . . . I never got around to it. . . ." was his only explanation.

Too bad, too, because that laziness and indifference cost him close to $600. Maybe it was worth it to him. But if *your* budget won't allow for such extravagance, this chapter will show you how to make friends with your car and, as a result, receive from it many years and thousands of miles more service—all for probably less money pro rated over a very few years than it's now costing to keep your car running. Most of these preventive measures won't cost you any more than a few minutes in time each week—and very little in money.

The only requisite for this insurance is a willingness to get better acquainted with your car and its needs. In the preceding chapter we described how a car works. Now we're going to discuss what to do to keep it running and performing in peak condition permanently.

Regular maintenance is not only a front-line defense against later costly repairs, it's also among your best defenses against any kind of auto-repair fraud. How? Simple, actually. If you are alert to your car's service needs and keep a record of all maintenance, you're not likely to be fooled when some shyster tries to convince you that the plugs need replacing. Not if you know they were changed in the last 5000 miles or so.

By now you have a working knowledge of how a car operates. The next step is to put this information to some practical use. Carry this book with you in your car, and refer to it regularly. Spend a couple of hours one day going over your car—slowly—trying to identify each part. There will undoubtedly be quite a few of them you won't recognize, but you'll probably be surprised at just how many you *can* identify. If you have a regular mechanic, ask him to point out what's what, or check with him if you're not sure about something. Most mechanics, if they're not too busy, are more than willing to help someone learn about cars. After you've become more familiar with your car's anatomy, begin reading the rest of this chapter and follow the suggestions we've made—all based on expert recommendations.

The Body and Chassis

Never underestimate the value and importance of washing and waxing a car. A clean car not only looks better, it really *does* run better. Road film and the normal accumulation of dirt inside and out are major causes of wear and deterioration of everything from paint and chrome to seat covers and carpeting.

Wash your car once a week—summer and winter. Especially in winter since water washes away corroding substances like salt. In winter the time to worry most about corrosion is when the temperature hovers in the 30-degree range. That's when snow melts and mixes with salt to attack the metal.

Water causes rust. Mud and caked-on dust are excellent places for water to accumulate. Such accumulations make it important to wash your car regularly. Washing is particularly important during inclement weather, even though you know the car is going to get dirty again before you've driven more than a few blocks. It is also a good idea, when possible, to squirt water from a high-pressure hose on the underside and up in and around the wheels to wash away accumulations of salt, road grime, grease, and mud. This is an added defense against premature rusting of such vital parts as drive-line joints, springs, shocks, brake lines and cables, and dozens of other important components.

Another advantage to regular washing and cleaning is that you spot scrapes, scratches, and chips soon after they happen. Wherever the paint is broken, rusting will start unless the area is sealed immediately. Touching up is an easy task—with the correct paint. If rusting has already started, rub it off with steel wool. Remember: *Painting over rust is a waste of time! The rust will continue to thrive and spread under that coat of cosmetic paint.*

Chrome polish should be used regularly on the bumpers and any trim as protection against rust and deterioration. Chrome cleaners are often excellent agents for removing rust and grime, but be careful before using them on any aluminum trim. Always wash your car thoroughly before waxing it. A mild dish-washing detergent or some of the car cleaners now on the market will help you do a more thorough job.

Most waxes today have cleaning agents already in them, making it unnecessary to use both a cleaner and a wax. Liquid waxes are usually much easier to apply and buff out, but the paste variety, which is harder to buff, will give your car better protection for a longer time. Deciding which to use is strictly a matter of personal preference. It simply boils down to this: Use lots of elbow grease and only wax your car twice a year (spring and fall) or take it easy and face the job about every three months.

You can quickly tell if your car is in need of a wax job by hosing it off for a few minutes and then watching to see if the water beads up. If it doesn't, better buy some wax and schedule a couple of hours on your next day off.

The inside of your car can be kept in good condition for years with much less work than is necessary on the exterior. Two rubber floor mats give excellent protection to the carpets. A vacuum cleaner is the best weapon against unnecessary and premature wear of carpets and seat covers. Even vinyl seats need vacuuming to rid them of bits of sand and dirt that wedge into the seams; the resulting grinding action wears out threads and leads to splitting and bursting of seat covers.

Unless there are stains (in which case, consult your owner's manual) you can do an excellent cleaning job on seats, instrument panel, and doors with a cloth dampened in warm water containing a few drops of vinegar. Use the same solution and cloth on the inside of the windows to clean off the buildup of film, particularly from cigarette smoke. You'll be amazed at the results.

Tired of those little but irritating squeaks and rattles? A small can of lubricant squirted into door locks and around door and trunk hinges every three months or so will miraculously reduce most or all of those pesky noises.

The Engine

Possibly the best protection you can give your engine is a regular oil change. In most U.S. cars built since the early 1960s, the engine oil needs to be changed every four months or 6000 miles, whichever comes first. Learn how to use the dipstick. You'll get the most accurate reading when the engine is cold. The safe reading is above the "add" mark and below the "full" mark. Don't overfill the engine with oil; it can cause serious problems.

The oil filter should be replaced every other oil change. Oil picks up dirt and other abrasive materials. And since the oil filter traps these impurities, it is vital to your car's lubrication system. It does, however, have a limited life. Once it's clogged up, it's useless. The oil will then bypass the filter altogether, and the abrasive particles will begin rapidly eating away at the engine.

If you notice an oil leak where your car is parked, have a mechanic check the gasket between the oil filter and the engine housing and also the gasket between the rocker arm cover and cylinder head. It's a good idea to tell the mechanic to clean the engine first, since it's difficult to find an oil leak on a dirt-encrusted engine but quite easy when the engine is clean.

In order to do its job, the oil has to be brought to an efficient operating temperature; and it has to be pumped to every part of the engine. In cold weather, let the engine idle for about a minute before driving off, but don't let it idle excessively. This wastes gas and builds sludge and carbon. Never "gun" a cold engine. After starting, especially in winter, drive the first few miles at a reasonably slow speed to let the engine reach its optimum temperature. And never accelerate in neutral just before turning the engine off. By accelerating, you're not priming the engine properly for the next time you start. You're merely washing the vital oil film off the cylinder walls with wasted gasoline.

In addition to its protective qualities, oil is directly related to engine efficiency. And efficient operation is directly related to gas mileage. Oil, in the correct amount and weight, cuts down on internal friction and helps carry away engine heat. Where a warm engine (operating at 180 to 190 degrees) is an efficient engine, too much heat (such as from internal friction), can be an engine's worst enemy. Running an engine too low on oil, or with the wrong kind of oil, can affect gasoline mileage as well as ultimate engine life.

It would probably astonish most car owners and more than a few mechanics if they knew how many racing drivers use 20W oil in their crankcases. Light oil allows an engine to warm up more quickly and helps reduce drag that dilutes power. You can increase engine efficiency by changing from heavy oil (40W or over) to a lighter weight. More than 90 percent of all cars on the highway can use a good 10W-30 oil. This cuts internal drag, thus increasing gas mileage. Your car's engine will also warm up quicker—and the sooner the better for good gas mileage.

One more important thing about lubrication. If the oil-pressure warning light comes on while you're driving, stop immediately and find out what's wrong. Continuing to drive with low oil pressure can ruin the engine.

The Cooling System

Equally important for engine protection is the cooling process. We've already discussed the mixing of water and coolant for better cooling and protection against rust and corrosion. In addition, you should check the coolant level in the radiator at least once a week. The radiator pressure cap used on modern cars should be inspected and tested at least once a year. It's holding down water and steam under pressure, and this pressure puts a heavy strain on the radiator and heater hoses. That's why you should also check the hoses regularly and have them replaced as soon as they show signs of wear. See that the fan belt is checked regularly for wear and tension. If you do it yourself, be sure to switch off the engine!

The entire cooling system should be drained and flushed out every two years. This will give you added protection against the buildup of rust and corrosion that will shorten the life of an engine by many thousands of miles. Here's another valuable tip. Modern engines run more efficiently (and use less gas) if heat is maintained within a certain range. The upper limit of this range is the point at which the engine runs most efficiently. If the cooling system of your car is in good shape, with no leaks and with fairly new rubber hoses, and if the pressure cap on the radiator is working correctly, remove the old thermostat and install one rated from 180 to 195 degrees. Since the function of the thermostat is to restrict the flow of water in the system until it reaches a certain temperature, the new one will cause the engine to run hotter by restricting the flow until heat causes it to open.

If your car's engine begins overheating during stop and go traffic on a hot day, turn on the heater. This may warm you up a little but it will cool down the engine a lot. However, if the red warning light stays on, stop the car, switch off the engine, and open the hood. But *do not* touch the radiator cap while the engine is hot. After about 20 or 30 minutes you can add water if necessary, assuming it's available. Otherwise, drive to the nearest gas station to have the system checked.

If you're ever caught by a surprise freeze without sufficient antifreeze in your car, take off the radiator cap before starting. If the coolant is still liquid, you can start the car. If it's slushy, cover the radiator and run the engine for three or four minutes; then shut it off and let the heat penetrate. Repeat this until the coolant has completely thawed. Remember to be careful each time you release that radiator cap.

The Electrical System

The most important thing you can do to avoid electrical problems is to keep the battery, which is the key to the entire system, properly maintained. But be very careful. The fluid in the battery is a combination of sulphuric acid and water, and the battery generates explosive gases. An exposed flame or a spark near the battery can cause an explosion. If battery acid comes in contact with your skin, it will cause a painful burn. Splashed in the eyes, it can cause permanent damage—even blindness.

The most important thing about battery maintenance is keeping the fluid topped off and the terminals clean. The fluid should be checked at least once a month, once a week in hot weather. Distilled water is recommended; tap water can be used unless it has a very heavy mineral content. Check with your mechanic or just use distilled water, which is the best idea anyway. Then you don't have to worry.

If the battery uses too much water, have the alternator and voltage regulator checked; they may be overcharging and damaging the battery. To protect the battery and to be sure it delivers the current when you need it, you should have it cleaned twice a year. If you do the job yourself, cover the vent holes and use a thick mixture of water and baking soda. Swab it around with a small brush. After it has set for about half an hour, rinse off the mixture with clear water. To avoid the buildup of corrosion, periodically apply a small amount of grease or petroleum jelly to each terminal.

Have your mechanic check the tension regularly on the V belt which drives the alternator or generator. Replace it immediately if it's cracked or worn. If it breaks while you're driving, trouble is not far ahead. The engine will begin drawing all its current from the battery, which will quickly run down and leave you without any electrical current.

Spark plugs have much more to do with engine efficiency and fuel economy than most drivers realize. A single spark plug misfiring can cost one full mile out of every ten you travel! Generally, a spark-plug defect can be noted when the engine is under load, that is, accelerating to pass or when climbing a steep grade. You might then notice a miss. A malfunction in the distributor points can generally be assumed if the engine misses under a light load, such as steady driving. For maximum performance and economy (which is becoming increasingly important to us all), spark plugs should be cleaned, checked, and regapped every 5000 or 6000 miles for most efficient service; they should be replaced at about double that mileage.

The Fuel and Exhaust System

An inoperative or clogged smog (PCV) system can make an engine drink gasoline like a thirsty horse in the desert. Cleaning or replacing the check valve is sufficient on the "open" system on earlier-model cars. But the "closed" system on most cars today features hose connections between the rocker arm cover and the intake manifold (or the air cleaner) and between the carburetor air cleaner and the oil filler cap. These hoses should be checked periodically by a mechanic. Since state and federal laws govern smog-control systems around the country, it may be illegal for you to fool with this yourself—and certainly unwise unless you're a fairly skilled mechanic. Just check these hoses for signs of wear or have a mechanic inspect them.

Another small but vital element in your fuel system is the fuel filter. Make sure that it's replaced at the recommended intervals. A clogged fuel filter will restrict the flow of gasoline. The filter in the air cleaner also needs replacing or cleaning at regular intervals. How often, of course, depends on where you live. If much of your driving is on dirt roads in rural areas, the filter may need cleaning or replacing every six months. Sometimes heavy city driving with its smog and other pollutants is just as demanding on the service of the air filter. Whatever your particular driving situation, keep the air filter clean. If it's dirty and clogged, your gasoline mileage can drop by as much as *50 percent.* The reason is that the dirtier the filter, the richer the mixture since less air enters the engine. A dirty air filter can cause even more serious and expensive problems. The carburetor and engine both may be damaged, and engine performance is certain to suffer.

You can remove the filter element by unscrewing the wing nut on top and in the center of the air-cleaner housing—that big round metal thing sitting on top of the engine. It's usually only finger-tight, so when you put it back in place, just tighten it with your fingers. Lift the filter element out and examine it. Hold it up to the light and try to see through it. If the filter is dirty, it might be saved by tapping it on a concrete floor, carefully knocking out the accumulation of dirt. Or, you can try blowing it clean with an air hose. Just be sure that you blow from the inside out and that you don't get the air hose close enough to tear the filter paper. Once the paper is torn, the filter is worthless and must be replaced. When you reinstall the filter, either the used one you've cleaned or a new one, be sure it's properly seated in the housing. Then put the lid back on the air cleaner and tighten the wing nut. This is one of those many simple maintenance tasks you can perform yourself, getting better acquainted with your car and saving a few pennies at the same time. There will also be less chance of some unscrupulous repairman selling you something you don't need.

The automatic choke, as you know, provides the carburetor with a very rich mixture when the engine is starting from cold. It's a good idea to have a mechanic check the automatic choke occasionally to see that it's operating properly. When it's not, it can cause much grief in cold-weather starting. An inefficient choke also wastes gasoline.

Brakes

You cannot create or destroy energy. You can only trade. Braking creates friction, and energy is passed off in the form of heat. But that's the energy you paid for in the form of gasoline to keep your car in motion, and it's wasted. All of us have to make panic stops in emergency situations, but you can avoid hard use of your brakes by always driving as far ahead as possible. It'll save gas. Many drivers are constantly losing motion by repeated and frequent application of their brakes simply because they don't plan ahead. Try to avoid last-minute braking for corners and turns. On a city street, you can and should be aware of traffic a full half-block ahead. On the open highway, you should be able to judge things up to a quarter of a mile.

Using your brakes wisely can not only save you money in improved gas mileage, but also in repair bills. All you need to do to earn some of these money-saving benefits is to pay a little more attention to what you're doing when you're driving. For example, driving with a dragging parking brake can cost you in both gasoline economy and wear. If the brake lever is only partially off, you could be pressing the rear-brake shoes gently into the drum. Always be sure it's completely off before you drive away. Don't count on the brake warning light; it sometimes goes off an instant before the brake is fully released.

It's also possible that the parking-brake cable (a mechanical connection rather than hydraulic) is just tight enough to cause the rear brakes to drag even if the brake lever is fully released. The cable is easy to spot when the car is up on a hoist. See that there is a bit of slack in it when the handle is fully released. The cable will run from each rear wheel to a common point, then on to the handle. A turnbuckle is normally provided for adjustment.

Riding the brake pedal is another bad habit of too many motorists. This is both dangerous and costly. If you ride the brakes, you not only wear them down quicker, but you also create drag that the engine must overcome. You're taxing it with a bigger load. Since this is extra drag, you must use extra gas. By riding the brake you are making the body of the car seem heavier to the engine than it really is. You could get the same effect by mounting an economy-car engine in the frame of a luxury car. The small engine would be forced to work much harder to get the job done. Even worse, there is the distinct possibility that the driver behind you might misread your brake lights.

Experts say some drivers are completely unaware that their foot is resting on the brake pedal as they drive. Check yourself. You could be losing gas and wearing out your car's brakes without even knowing it.

Sometimes, because of a misadjustment, the brake shoes will drag just slightly without your resting your foot on the brake pedal. You might not even notice this slight dragging as you drive, but the friction is steadily pulling against the thrust of the engine. An easy test you can make yourself is to see that all wheels turn freely when the car is on a hoist. If they're dragging, any service-station attendant can adjust the brakes for about $2.50. Most disc-brake pads are mounted to be in slight contact with the rotor when they are correctly adjusted. So if your car has disc brakes, don't worry if there appears to be a slight drag.

Although wheel bearings aren't directly related to the brakes, they are vitally important to fuel economy and safety. Friction in wheel bearings can not only lead to short bearing life and costly repairs, it can also reduce gas mileage considerably. Rear-wheel bearings are normally lubricated automatically and need little or no attention, but front-wheel bearings should be inspected and repacked every 15,000 miles. This job should cost no more than $10.

The best reason for taking care of your brakes is that your life depends on them. Start by reading what your owner's manual has to say, and follow its recommendations carefully. Make a habit of constantly checking the braking system, starting with the brake pedal. If there's too much pedal travel, drive back and forth several times in someplace like an empty parking lot, braking firmly to let the self-adjusting mechanism adjust the shoes. If this doesn't work, or if the pedal has a "spongy" feeling, have the brakes checked at once. Brakes should also be checked *without delay* if the car pulls to one side or the other when you apply them or if you hear *any* unusual noises when braking, turning, or parking.

See that the fluid level in the master cylinder is checked at the recommended intervals by your regular mechanic or at a service station. Leaks can also occur in the brake line; and if you drive a car that's over three years old, you should insist on a careful check of the entire length of the brake lines. On older cars it's excellent insurance to either have the master cylinder overhauled or replaced.

If you hear a scraping noise coming from the brakes when you apply them, it's a signal that the shoes are scraping and damaging the drums—and that you're probably in for a big repair bill. You can avoid letting the situation get that far, however, if you have the brakes checked and adjusted by a competent mechanic once a year. It will be more than worth the expense and trouble in terms of safety and the prevention of costly (and unnecessary) repairs later.

Tires

Like the brakes, tires can save your life. Not surprisingly, tire failure is one of the main causes of auto accidents. Safety experts across the country agree that negligence on the part of drivers—rather than poor product quality—is the major cause of tire failure. The number-one culprit, says the California Highway Patrol, is excessive wear.

Tires should be replaced as soon as possible when they have only 1/16 of an inch of tread or when the sidewall is damaged enough to expose or separate the cords. The same is true whenever a bulge or any kind of separation becomes visible.

Tires, suspension, and steering are all interrelated, and trouble in any one of these areas may affect the other two. That's why it's impossible to get good tire mileage unless you keep your front wheels properly aligned and all your wheels properly balanced. Worn shock absorbers will cause your car to wander about the road, and wandering wastes fuel and rubber. Bad shocks can also cause wheel-alignment problems, which also shortens the life of tires.

To make sure you don't neglect air pressure, keep the tires inflated according to manufacturer's recommendations. Both underinflation and overinflation reduce tire life drastically.

The front and rear tires do different jobs, they wear at different rates, and if the spare is unused, it gets no wear at all. You'll enjoy a better ride and get improved tire mileage by having the tires rotated approximately every 6000 miles. With the different tire constructions available today, however, be careful not to mix them. Radials should be used only in complete sets of four. *Never use two different constructions on the same axle.*

Most new cars today come equipped with radial tires. Not only are radials exceptionally safe and good for longer mileage before they must be replaced, they also help improve gas mileage. As a matter of fact, you can expect an increase of up to about six percent with radials. Because of their soft sidewall but very firm, hard tread-area construction, they roll over the pavement with less wiggle and squirm, and thus less friction, than bias-ply tires. Some tire companies claim an increase in gas mileage of ten percent, but we believe that increases beyond six percent will vary depending on driving techniques and conditions.

Keep in mind if you peruse the tire market that a change to larger tires has the same effect as changing to a lower rear-axle ratio. This increases gasoline mileage, but fender clearance may limit the size of tire you can use. Should you decide to change, be very sure a larger tire will fit in all turning situations.

Wheel Alignment and Balancing

Correct wheel alignment and wheel balance are essential to safe and comfortable steering. If the wheels are not properly aligned and balanced, they can also reduce the life of your tires by half—or more. If your car's wheels pull to the right or left on a straight road, you may need a wheel alignment. If the steering wheel vibrates, have the wheels checked for balance. When you have a new tire fitted it's always well worth the small extra charge to have it balanced right then and there.

Remember, however, that the rough and careless driver can never depend on his car's wheels staying balanced and properly aligned. All it takes to mess things up is to hit a hole hard or bump the curb. If you can't avoid hitting a chuckhole in the road, at least slow down and remove your foot from the brake just before you do in order to reduce the shock to the suspension and wheels.

Tuneups

Considering its complexity, the speed at which it operates, and the continual punishment it takes, it's indeed amazing that your car's engine works as well and lasts as long as it does. Proper maintenance makes a big difference, too. With regular tuneups, your engine will give better gas mileage, run more efficiently, and be much less likely to stall or let you down. That means two tuneups a year or every 12,000 miles; a minor tuneup, preferably in the spring, and a complete tuneup in the late fall. Engine tuneups vary in scope, depending on whether they are major or minor, but the following will give you a good idea of the main adjustments, tests, and replacements the mechanic should perform in a complete tuneup.

Spark plugs will be either cleaned or replaced. After carefully examining the ignition cables, the mechanic will install new points and replace the condenser.

The battery will be checked with a voltmeter.

The mechanic will use a compression gauge to test the amount of compression in each of the cylinders. Low readings could indicate expensive repairs, including new piston rings and work on the valves.

The ignition timing will be checked to make sure the spark is occurring at precisely the right moment. This is accomplished with a *timing light,* which is an electronic device used to align the timing marks on the engine with the electrical current sent out by the distributor. The spark coming from the distributor is then either advanced or retarded as necessary.

The mechanic will then inspect the fuel pump to make certain it's in good operating condition. The fuel filter also will be either cleaned or replaced. The air filter also should be checked to see if it needs cleaning or replacing. For better performance and gasoline economy, the carburetor idle mixture is adjusted, and the automatic choke (if your car is so equipped) is checked and adjusted.

Drive belts will be examined for wear and checked for tension with a special tension gauge.

Emission control systems vary according to the car and model year, but it's vital for engine efficiency and cleaner air that they function properly. The PCV valve is replaced, and the hoses and other parts of the system are cleaned and inspected.

The cost of tuneups varies considerably from engine to engine, garage to garage, and even area to area, depending on labor rates. The expense of such maintenance, however, is more than offset by improved engine efficiency and longevity—that is, if you intend to keep the car for more than three years. If you trade off every two or three years, don't bother. You'll never see a return on the investment you make in maintenance beyond required factory service under the warranty. (The crucial time for deciding whether to pour more money into the old car or to trade it in on a newer model is at around 60,000 miles, according to studies made by the U.S. Department of Transportation. Repair needs seem to hit their peak at about that mileage. If you prefer repair bills, however, to payments, the study shows that it's still cheaper on a per-mile cost basis to keep the old car.)

You can also save even more money by investing in the necessary tools and equipment for the job and performing your own tuneups. The money you save would easily pay for the investment in tools within two years or even less. Therefore, if you're even slightly mechanically minded and want to learn how to take better care of your car or are simply eager to save money, it's certainly worth considering. Most high schools and junior colleges throughout the country today offer excellent adult courses in auto mechanics that are worth many times the small tuition charge. They're certainly worth investigating. One friend, tired of being ignorant of cars and at the mercy of dishonest mechanics, took such a course and now regularly performs all her own maintenance—from lube jobs to major tuneups. And her increased knowledge has already saved her from the unscrupulous. When one mechanic told her the heavy carbon deposits on the spark plugs in her car signaled the need for a major tuneup, she laughed and told him it only indicated that the mixture was too rich. The $15 course she took is already paying big dividends.

Winterizing Your Car

Winter weather is hard on your car—the engine, suspension, and cooling system in particular. You can protect your car and yourself by following a few "winterizing" routines and setting an early deadline for getting the job done. A list of what to do follows.

The battery is your first line of defense against such winter woes as a hard-starting car. Inspect, test, and, if necessary, replace the battery. Make sure it's free of corrosion.

Inspect the radiator hoses and connections, for they are common trouble spots during winter months. If they appear at all worn, replace them. Check the coolant, and drain and flush the system or add antifreeze if necessary.

Inspect the brakes, master cylinder, and brake lines for leaks and top off the fluid if required.

Lubricate the chassis, change the oil (keeping in mind the correct seasonal grade), and change the oil filter.

Now's the perfect time for getting that tuneup we just described. Your engine will need all the help you can give it in order to perform its job in winter.

Check the exhaust system for leaks or any damage. During winter is when the exhaust system is most likely to fail; and since you do more driving with all the windows rolled up, it becomes a major safety hazard.

Inspect the windshield wipers and replace them if necessary. Also check the windshield washer and defroster. (You might also consider installing a rear-window defroster which is a tremendous asset in winter.)

Mount the snow tires and have the wheels balanced.

In addition to winterizing your car, there are a few additional and simple precautions you can take that will make winter driving both a little easier and a lot safer. Carry a sturdy, long-handled scraper-brush, a flashlight, and a set of flares. Before you start off, remove snow and ice from all the windows. During icy conditions, let the engine warm up sufficiently for the defrosters to do their work. Use the windshield washer regularly while driving on sloppy roads. When you stop, shut off the wipers before turning off the engine in order to prevent them from freezing to the windshield. If this happens, the wiper motor will burn out the next time you start the car.

Gas-Saving Techniques

As fuel prices continue to soar, good gas mileage becomes increasingly important to us all. A well-running car is always the first step in getting better gas mileage, but good driving habits can add considerably to mileage savings and reduce wear. Following are a few techniques you can employ each day that will put money back in your pocket for things other than gasoline and car repairs.

Don't start the engine until you're ready to go. Say your goodbyes and check your maps *before* starting the engine. Don't warm it needlessly. Every moment you sit without moving while the engine is idling you are wasting gas. Thirty seconds should be long enough to get oil moving in a cold engine; a warm engine is ready to go immediately. *Shut off the engine when you stop.* There's a popular myth insisting that you should allow the engine to idle rather than turning the ignition off and starting it up again, since starting takes so much gas. This may be true if you're only stopping at a signal or a stop sign, but tests have shown that if you plan to sit in one place for more than about one minute, you should, when practical, of course, shut off the engine. Any idling time over one minute will burn up more gasoline than restarting the engine.
Drive at a steady speed when at all possible or practical. The chart below is from a study made by the U.S. Department of Transportation, and indicates that very slow speeds do not necessarily mean better gas mileage.

Speed	Miles per Gallon
30 mph	15.61
40 mph	14.89
50 mph	16.98
60 mph	13.67
70 mph	11.08

The following results were obtained in a survey conducted by the Automobile Club of Southern California and indicate the value of steady driving.

Steady freeway driving......................... 17 miles per gallon
Street driving in light traffic .... 15 miles per gallon
Street driving in heavy traffic .... 9 miles per gallon

Drive well ahead of yourself. The idea here is to be well aware of everything happening far ahead. Then adjust your speed and driving to the situation.

Pass other cars smoothly and carefully. Wait and watch. Study the road ahead until you have ample room to pass safely with steady acceleration; then press down on the gas pedal slowly and smoothly. Make the entire operation smooth and you'll conserve gasoline.

Avoid "jackrabbit" starts. There's always a great temptation to use that horsepower under our command when we're at the wheel of a car. But there are few driving practices that gobble up both gasoline and rubber faster than rapid getaways.

Take it easy when climbing hills. There is a point at which the engine is most efficient. Beyond this point, fuel is wasted. Where is this point? It varies from car to car, of course, but you'll be able to feel it. It's when you step down a little harder on the accelerator and there isn't any significant difference in speed. If you have a chance to study the hill before reaching it, try to anticipate and gradually increase your speed up to the legal limit while you're still on level ground. Speed costs much less in gas consumption on level road. You can use the extra velocity to help climb part of the way up the hill.

Change lanes carefully. Here's a typical situation. A car is moving along immediately to your right just when you want to move to that lane to exit the freeway. The temptation is always to surge forward and move in ahead of that car, right? Resist the temptation. Just back off slightly and slip in behind the car. You'll save a measurable amount of gas and arrive at your destination only a few seconds later. It's well worth it.

Shift gears as soon as possible. Shifting too soon or too late costs you money in wasted gasoline. Too soon causes lugging or laboring, and too late uses needless lower gear power. With an automatic transmission, use a light touch on the gas pedal to encourage the transmission to shift into the next higher gear quickly. The shifting process in automatic transmissions is governed by the linkage pressure. So the harder you step on the gas, the longer the engine runs in a lower gear and the more fuel it consumes.

Minimize the use of air conditioners. Air conditioning places a substantial load on car engines. While driving at 30 mph, for example, using the air conditioner can cost you two miles per gallon. As a rule, use of an air conditioner cuts gasoline mileage by 10 percent. The reason is that your engine must devote up to 15 percent of its power to drive the system.

Minimize the load. Transporting unnecessary weight in your car will cause it to use more fuel. It also wears out the brakes sooner because they have to work harder and more often.

Lubricate the heat valve in the exhaust manifold. This valve, located in the exhaust system of some cars, allows exhaust gases to heat the intake manifold during cold-engine operation. A valve stuck in the open position causes slow engine warm-up and poor cold-engine performance. A valve stuck in the closed position will cause a loss of power and hard starting with a hot engine. Either way, you waste gasoline.

Maintain correct tire pressure. Improper tire inflation is the chief cause of excessive wear and can reduce the life of any tire by 25 percent. In terms of time and money that can mean buying tires six months sooner than necessary. Underinflated tires reduce gasoline mileage slightly; soft tires wear out quicker. Tires should not, however, be inflated above the maximum recommended pressure.

Form car pools. One of the best ways to conserve gasoline is to form car pools. Talk with friends, neighbors, and colleagues about taking one car to a common destination.

Chapter 8

What to Do if You Get Gypped

Even the wisest consumers get taken once in a while. Maybe it's just the law of averages. Whatever the reason, you don't necessarily have to write it off to experience. On the contrary, there are so many laws on the books today, along with legal-aid organizations and consumer groups, that there's really no excuse for accepting defeat without at least a fight. The secret is usually in knowing how to handle a situation and where to go for help if you need it. That's what this chapter is all about. Your legal defenses may be much better than you think.

The first thing to remember is that if you aren't satisfied with a service or a product, or think you've been gypped, register your complaint *immediately*. The longer you put it off, the less your chances of winning any kind of satisfaction. Always begin by assuming that an honest mistake was made by the person you're dealing with, even if this is obviously not the case. Don't charge into the office or garage like an angry lion. You'll have much better control of the situation—and enhance your chance of success—if you present your case calmly. After all, your goal should be to get satisfaction, not make enemies. Even if you eventually have to get tough, you'll be much more effective if you keep your cool. Let the other guy lose control, not you.

Consider writing down what you want to say and rehearse if necessary. That doesn't mean you should memorize lines and make a speech. But if you know what you want to say, you'll be much less likely to get flustered and begin stammering. Most of us are not naturally aggressive, nor do we have much experience at methodically wearing down someone who we feel has wronged us. We have a tendency to lash out emotionally and then leave. This may be great therapy, but it's not of much value in the business world.

Sometimes it's difficult to remain calm, especially if the person you're confronting jumps to the attack. You should be prepared for that also, for it does happen. Here's an example.

"He said I should have my brains taken out, buttered, and fed to the dogs."

That quote is from a sailor's complaint about his treatment at the hands of a car dealer and his salesmen.

"My husband is a fine, intelligent man, and he does not deserve to be called an s.o.b."

That was a woman's complaint about the same dealer.

"I remember him best as the grossly overweight architect with the Polish wife."

That's an excerpt from a letter by a repair-shop owner about a dissatisfied customer.

These are just a few examples of what might be encountered. Such instances are most certainly in the minority, but they do exist. Rudeness does not seem to be the rule in the car business as a whole. But it does appear to be the modus operandi of a small number of operators. The examples cited here pertain only to incidents in which there were witnesses or substantiating documents. The man told to feed his brains to the dogs was Joe D. Burris, a sailor attached to the destroyer *John S. McCain*. Burris was trying to get back a $20 deposit he had put on a car with the understanding, he said, that he could get a refund if he changed his mind.

Burris spoke to two salesmen. At first, he wrote to the District Attorney, they tried to talk him into taking another car. Then they offered him a girl—a girl "who'll do anything you want." Then came their final offer—the girl plus a case of beer.

Burris protested, and told the salesmen that all he wanted was a refund, nothing else. That's when things got nasty.

"Salesman No. 1 repeatedly called me a flake, an s.o.b., and stupid. He specifically said I should have my brains taken out, buttered, and fed to the dogs. He said I was nothing but a flake, a stupid sailor who didn't know what he wanted. I just stood there. I couldn't believe that this was a salesman who was talking to me."

The young sailor finally left the dealer's lot, without his refund. The same dealer was the subject of a complaint by Mrs. Nelson Hunt, who says she tried for three months, with letters and telephone calls, to get the windshield-wiper motor repaired. Finally she obtained one herself from a different source and made an appointment with the dealer for installation.

"We spent the entire day there but the service department couldn't make the motor work," says Mrs. Hunt. "Before we left, we tried to explain our frustration to the owner and the manager. We were called names, yelled at, and told that they would take care of it when it was convenient. My husband is a fine, intelligent man, and he does not deserve to be called an s.o.b."

Abuse can sometimes be more than verbal.

The District Attorney of San Diego has a file on a case in which a dealer, after an argument with a customer over repairs, simply pulled the wire out of the coil in the customer's car. The customer, according to the file, had to call a policeman to get his coil wire back.

Too often vindictiveness is a little more subtle. The remark about the "grossly overweight architect with the Polish wife" was made by the president of a chain of car-repair shops. It was contained in a postscript to a letter to the District Attorney's office of a major U.S. city in which the dealer answered a repair complaint by the architect. This businessman, against whom a large file has accumulated in the District Attorney's office, appears to specialize in postscripts designed to embarrass or degrade any complainants. He ended another letter, this one to the Attorney General's office concerning a customer unhappy with a $427 repair bill for an oil leak, with this notation: "I also furnished him with a free car while we were repairing his. He returned it in extremely dirty condition."

Still another postscript—this one in a letter to a customer who reported he had had an accident due to brake failure after a brake overhaul. "When you left on your last visit here, you were observed by several employees making two illegal U-turns. It might be well for you to review your driving practices in the interest of safety to yourself and others."

The customer in this case, however, had the last word—a kind of post-postscript. A small-claims court awarded him $300, plus costs against the dealer.

Chances are slim that you'll ever encounter this kind of abuse, especially if you handle the situation properly. But you should always be prepared for a bitter fight, just in case. Time consuming as it may be, it's always best to use the chain of command. Speak first with the mechanic who did the work or the salesman you dealt with. This way you're at least giving them a chance to correct things without looking bad in front of the boss. If that doesn't work, then go to the next man on the command ladder.

If you're lucky, and the garage is reasonable, just voicing a simple complaint may be all you'll have to do to get the situation straightened out. But if verbal diplomacy isn't enough, the tactics you employ next may depend on the type of facility you're dealing with.

Specialty Shops and Service Stations

Track down the owner or franchise holder, and appeal to him as an independent businessman. Take the approach that you're sure he's as interested in setting things straight as you are and that probably he's quite disturbed that it wasn't done right the first time. Don't act as if you suspect him of being a crook. Your tone and choice of words can have as much effect on the results as anything. Don't sound patronizing either. Approach the problem in a positive frame of mind, and chances are that the outcome will mirror your attitude.

If you do encounter a stubborn owner who balks at your complaint, however, you'll need further prods. Write a letter to the local licensing board. Mechanics and salespersons may not be licensed, but businesses are. Most businessmen don't want to risk an investigation by the city and will work out the dispute, usually, in order to clear a complaint off the record.

Make your letter brief and pointed. Rambling and making disparaging remarks won't get you anywhere. This holds true whether the problem is unsatisfactory auto repair or questionable sales practices.

If none of these tactics works, take your complaint to the oil company or franchiser that controls the local facility. You should also send a copy to the Federal Trade Commission, which investigates franchisers and their business policies, and the local office of the Better Business Bureau. Make a notation at the bottom of the letter listing where copies were sent. Don't expect too much from the BBB, however. This is basically an organization of local businessmen, and its main purpose is to protect its members and keep fly-by-night operators out of town. There are a few exceptions, but generally the BBB answers inquiries from the public with such stock replies as "We've had no complaints against them" (which doesn't tell you much) or "They cooperate with us" (which translates to mean the business in question pays its dues). There are signs, however, that the BBB, or at least some of its branches, is taking more initiative in consumer protection. These efforts are long overdue, but still appreciated.

Car Dealerships

Your initial approach to a complaint should be about the same with any kind of operation. At new-car dealerships, however, you may well face a considerable amount of bureaucratic red tape that could send you spinning. Once you have registered your complaint with the service manager, your next move—if you don't get satisfaction—is to bypass the various functionaries and head directly for the president or owner. By doing so you brand yourself as a customer who is determined to get his or her money's worth and isn't going to give up. Always be polite, but not apologetic. After all, you aren't begging favors, only demanding what you paid for.

Once you've presented your case to the owner and are reasonably convinced you're not going to get any satisfaction, your next step is to contact the zone or district manager. Your owner's manual should list the addresses of zone managers. Nearly all car makers, both American and foreign, use some form of the district representative system. It won't do any good to go directly to the manufacturer because he will simply send the letter back to the district or zone manager, and your complaint will be further delayed.

If the problem relates to safety or the possibility of considerable damage if the situation isn't corrected immediately, you should consider making a phone call. Most companies accept collect calls at the district offices. Some small companies stipulate that you pay for your own complaint call, but unless it's so stated in your owner's manual or service manual, call collect.

Although making a phone call is quicker, it's more difficult to compose your thoughts over the telephone, and the chance of your speaking with anyone more important than a secretary is slim anyway. For this reason, we recommend a letter unless the problem is genuinely urgent. In addition, should your letter fail to get satisfaction, you have positive proof with your carbon copy that you wrote without getting results. This will definitely help if you decide to take some form of legal action.

Independent Garages

You're less likely to get the runaround from independent shops than any other repair operation. This is mostly because there are fewer people to deal with, and the independent is most likely sincerely interested in pleasing customers. Also, you probably will be able to chat with the owner himself. And dealing with someone who can make a decision is almost always a simple matter.

If you do run into trouble, follow about the same procedure we described in dealing with specialty shops or service stations. Write a letter to the local licensing board, the BBB, and the Independent Garage Owners of America if the shop involved is a member of that nationwide organization. This is a group of conscientious repairmen with strong sanctions against members who fail to adhere to their code of ethics.

Turning to the Media

In many cities and towns around the country today newspapers and television stations have consumer reporters who help people with problems by acting as intermediaries. All it usually takes for you to enlist this aid is to write a letter describing your trouble in detail. The volume of mail received daily by the media from disgruntled consumers prohibits them from publishing or broadcasting every letter. But each one should receive attention, and few businessmen want bad publicity. This course of action should only be followed, however, after you've failed to get results from the company itself. Give them the first chance to set things straight; then they won't have any gripe coming if you turn elsewhere for help.

The Complaint Letter

The best weapon in any consumer's arsenal is a good complaint letter. Correctly written, with copies sent to the proper places, it can often bring quick and even amazing results. Its success, however, depends mostly on how the letter explains the situation and who receives it.

A complaint letter should be a factual, well-organized account of what caused your grievance. Don't apologize or make threats; and don't worry about literary style and cleverness. Facts are what count. Don't dress them up to make your case sound better. Someone will eventually ferret out the truth, and he won't be happy about being misled. And your credibility will suffer. A typed letter is better than a hand-written one, but only because it's easier to read.

The complaint letter should include all of the following information.

Your name, address, and telephone number.
The name and address of the garage.
The make and model year of your car, and the warranty number if it's a warranty complaint.

A description of what happened, including dates, and what has been done to resolve the complaint.
A total of how much the dispute has cost you in money, time lost from work, alternative transportation (i.e., buses, cabs, etc.), and repairs made elsewhere.
Copies of the repair bill and any other relevant paper work or correspondence between you and the garage.

Without editorializing, write a brief description of what happened. The more personal criticism the letter contains, the less likely it will be taken seriously. So stick to the facts. If you think the person you dealt with was rude, say so, and explain why. Just avoid philosophizing and haranguing. Remember to keep a copy of your letter for your own records.

Here is an actual letter sent to the consumer column of a large daily newspaper. It serves as a good example of how to organize the facts and supply any investigators with enough solid information to enable them to judge whether or not there is a legitimate complaint. In this case, the consumer was obviously victimized by what at best could be described as shabby advertising and business practices.

Dear Sir:

I have a complaint against _____ for false advertisement and price misrepresentation by one of their salespeople.

On Saturday, 25 May, the price quoted me for a used 1973 Toyota, license number 819HQC, was $2900.00. I told him it was overpriced. That night in the classified ads the same car was advertised for $2200.00.

Sunday, 26 May, I went to _____ again to ask about the car and this time I was told that it was for $2695.00 by the same salesman that told me the day before that it sold for $2900.00. When I showed him the ad from the paper, he became very violent. When I told him that the car is to be sold at the advertised price, and asked why he quoted two different prices, he became argumentative and profane.

As an agent for _____ he said he wasn't aware of the advertisement in the paper. Being a salesman he should know what the advertised price is before he arbitrarily quotes higher prices than advertised and what the car is worth.

The salesman also used obscene language to my wife and daughter and my 4-year-old granddaughter. In a loud voice he told my wife, who was standing quietly on the sidewalk to, quote, "Get your ass out of here." My daughter was offended by his language and told him so. Then he told her to also, "Get your ass out of here!" I told him to keep a civil tongue and he told me to "Get the hell off of my property!"

I then went to the sales office to tell his immediate boss the situation with the advertisement and the use of obscenities. He showed a lack of interest and threw me out of his office.

Is this the treatment I deserve after buying two new cars from _____ in the past three years? I've been pleased with my two cars and was looking for a third for my daughter.

I would like to know what action I can take against the salesman for price misrepresentation and false advertisement and obscenities. I feel that my wife's rights were violated and I am deeply offended by the lack of courtesy showed me, a good customer. And my daughter and little granddaughter deserve an apology.

Sincerely,
(Name Withheld)

Although this firm was investigated by the local district attorney, the man who wrote this letter never did receive an apology. This leads us to our next section.

Legal Avenues

If all else fails, you may still have a chance to square things in the courtroom. But whatever happens, never threaten a lawsuit, even if you seriously plan on following through. Roughly 99 out of 100 people who threaten legal action never go any further than the threat. Most businessmen know this because they hear such empty threats frequently. Especially dishonest ones. So you're not going to scare any gyp artist with those tactics. Most consumers don't go that far because they either can't afford a lawyer or don't really want to make the effort. Besides, hiring a lawyer will usually cost more than the damages in most cases. Businessmen also know this.

In many cities, however, there is a method of suing which will cost you only a few dollars; and if you win, it costs *nothing*, except a little work. You can take your case to small-claims court. This is an informal court where a plaintiff or defendant doesn't need a lawyer. In fact, many of these courts bar lawyers altogether. You simply state your own case, the defendant states his position, and the judge asks questions and makes his decision.

The amount you can sue for is limited. It varies from as little as $100 in South Carolina to $5000 in Maryland; but the general limit is around $500, which is just about right for most auto-repair disputes.

Small-claims court was created in 1938 for the very purpose of providing a low-cost method of resolving minor disputes. Court is conducted in a highly informal manner. Legal expertise is not necessary, and judges usually lean over backwards to give both sides the benefit of their knowledge.

Although lawyers are not necessary in small-claims action, it's always wise to get some legal advice first. This small investment (usually around $25) is a good one, because if you muff your first chance, you won't get another. There is no appeal for the plaintiff in small-claims court. If you sue somebody and you win, he can appeal. But if you sue and lose, that's it. No appeal is possible for you. Only the defendant may appeal. This sometimes defeats the purpose of small-claims court. A businessman who loses a case in small claims can drag the appeals out all the way to the Supreme Court of the United States, and not too many consumers can afford to keep up with that.

But despite these pitfalls, small claims is still often your best bet if you can't find satisfaction any other way. The cost of filing a suit in small claims court is deliberately low, usually only a few dollars. You go to the court clerk's office, fill out a short form, and pay the small fee (generally around $5 to $15). The clerk sets a court date, usually within a few weeks. In some courts you can request an evening or Saturday session. A summons will then go via registered mail or by a court marshal to the party you're suing, notifying him that he must appear in court to answer your charges.

In taking your complaint to court you should locate all documents necessary to prove your case: estimates, repair bills, cancelled checks, and copies of letters. Are witnesses available? Someone who was with you or a mechanic who can offer expert opinion on the work performed. A written statement from a mechanic is usually enough.

The suit frequently ends with delivery of the summons. The party you're suing may take you more seriously then. An official court summons can do more than dozens of phone calls and letters. Out-of-court settlements are the rule rather than the exception in small-claims court. Another way you may prevail without an actual hearing is if the defendant doesn't show up in court. He may decide he doesn't want to lose the time at work or that he doesn't have a chance of convincing a judge he's in the right. In that case, the judge will look over the form you've filled out and review any supporting material, such as that mentioned above. Unless your case lacks any merit at all, you'll probably win by default; that is, the judge will rule in your favor and order the mechanic or garage to pay the money. Unless the mechanic has a good reason for missing the court appearance, he'll not be allowed to have the default judgment set aside.

If the defendant does show up, the judge will give you each about five minutes to tell your side of the story. This is why it's important for you to have all your supporting material organized. You might make an outline of what you want to say; it can serve as a guide to avoid leaving out any pertinent information. Don't read a statement. The hearing is more like a three-way conversation than a courtroom procedure. The whole session rarely takes longer than 30 minutes; 15 or 20 is about average.

Even if you win the judgment, the battle may not yet be won. The mere fact that a judge has awarded someone $500 is no guarantee that he'll get it. Getting the money is often the hardest part. The judgment is just a piece of paper that says you're entitled. Collecting is an entirely different matter.

To enforce payment, you'll first have to do some detective work on your own by finding out whether the debtor has any assets. Assets can be a house, a car, a bank account, or a paycheck, for example. Some assets are exempt from attachment, so it's best to find as many as possible. Armed with this list of assets, you go to the clerk of small-claims court and obtain a writ of execution (this costs around a dollar or two in most places), which you take to the marshal's office. Tell the marshal what you want him to go after. This also costs money, but the price depends on what the asset is. It ranges from about $5 for a wage or bank garnishment to a $150 deposit for attaching real property.

If the asset is money, the marshal will garnishee it. If it's property, he'll seize it and sell it at auction. In either case, you'll get your money. It may take time, but the wait may be worthwhile in terms of both money and satisfaction. (Asking for other expenses that are ordinarily incurred when your car is out of service, such as cab and bus fare, a rented car, and towing charges, is a good idea too. Some courts are now beginning to recognize these consequential damages.)

Both the stakes and the risks are much higher above the small-claims level. If you lose an action in regular court, it will cost you not only whatever the suit involves, but also attorney fees for your own lawyer and, possibly, the other party's counsel. Attorneys' fees alone scare off many clients. The starting point for handling a trial is around $300. That's rock bottom, and there is no ceiling. The average lawyer charges $40 to $50 an hour. The longer a case takes, the higher the fee.

Because of the cost, and the uncertainties of taking a case to court, lawyers will often advise their clients to settle for a negotiated compromise. The drawback to this is that the client usually gets much less than he might in a court judgment, and he must pay his lawyer out of his own pocket. The advantage is that there's no risk outside of the attorney fees. The cost of having your lawyer negotiate a settlement normally runs from $50 to $100, depending on how many letters he has to write.

Which of these courses of action the consumer follows is usually dictated by practical considerations—the amount of loss and the size of his bank account. But the law provides for more than mere recovery of one's loss. Civil codes generally provide for actual damages, injunctive relief, punitive damages, and any other remedy the court deems reasonable or proper.

"The amount of actual loss has no bearing on the action," explains one consumer lawyer. "A $200 dispute can result in a $200,000 judgment."

It's all a matter of how much perseverance the consumer has. The courts, however, are ruling more and more in favor of consumers, so—despite the expense—you may have a good chance of winning your case. But it could easily take two years or more, and that's what wears down or discourages so many consumers. You should always be prepared for a long and often tedious legal battle.

If you feel you've been defrauded by a repair shop, a complaint to state or local prosecutors could help lead to an investigation and the issuance of a criminal complaint against the garage. One major advantage of the criminal complaint is that it requires no lawyer and costs you nothing in terms of money. Your local prosecutor will file the charges for you. In most states a person filing a criminal complaint on auto repair must allege the following.

False pretenses (the mechanic knows he did not perform the work you were charged for).

Intent (he meant to cheat you).

The mechanic gained by his deception (he took your money).

You believed his false representations (by paying the bill).

As you can imagine, these are difficult charges to substantiate, and the penalties are often pitifully small. Still, it's worth your time to write or call the responsible law-enforcement officials in your city, county, and state. Some states are beefing up their consumer-fraud units in response to pressure from irate citizens and consumer groups.

Perhaps the consumer in the best financial position to take legal action, however, is the one with the least money. Poor people get free legal help. Anyone in a certain income bracket can find help from the Legal Aid Society, an organization funded by the Office of Economic Opportunity. Not only is the price right for these services, but the help is usually first class. Most lawyers working for legal-aid societies are young, gung-ho, and knowledgeable. Consumer cases are their daily diet. As one legal aid staffer in San Francisco put it, "Nobody, but *nobody* knows consumer law like poor people's lawyers."

Fighting Repossessions

Many a person wonders if a creditor can come onto his property in the middle of the night, hot-wire his car, and drive off in it. The answer is yes. Is it legal? Maybe.

Can he refuse to release any personal belongings in that car until he is paid in full? Sure he can. Is it legal? Probably not.

Can he seize a car which is worth more than the amount owed, sell it for less, and sue you for the difference? He can indeed. It may or may not be legal, but it happens every day.

"Unfortunately, the realities of the marketplace are sometimes governed not by legal niceties but by expediency," says Michael Weisz, legal-aid lawyer, consumer champion, authority on possession and repossession. "In the car business, the tendency is to establish possession first, and to worry about the rights and wrongs later."

Weisz does not dispute the moral and legal right of a businessman to reclaim merchandise when the buyer defaults on payments. But he believes there is too much room for abuse of this right. The law, or the absence of it, is weighted in favor of the creditor, he says, and against the consumer. There are three major reasons, Weisz says, why the consumer does not get a fair shake.

(1) Existing law is not explicit enough. Many questions on the legality of how repossessions may be handled have not been answered in court. "And as long as there are gray areas in the law, there'll be someone to exploit them."

(2) It's too easy for creditors and repossessors to ignore what law

there is. "A poor person whose car has been repossessed isn't likely to have the money for any legal action."

(3) Creditors have the unilateral right to declare that a default in payments exists and that a repossession is justified. "No legal process is required."

Never, during the normal course of a repossession, does a citizen have the opportunity to present his side to a legal arbiter before his car is taken. "The creditor does not have to give notice of intent to repossess," says Weisz. "He decides whether, when, where, and what. He plays the role of the court and of the marshal."

It was Weisz who won a landmark decision in U.S. District Court in California in 1972 declaring repossessions unconstitutional. The ruling was overturned in circuit court and now awaits the test of the U.S. Supreme Court. Until that court decides to rule on the matter and hands down a definitive judgment, repossessions remain the law of the land. The 14th Amendment to the U.S. Constitution holds that no state shall deprive a person of property without due process of law. The key phrase is "no state."

Creditors and repossessors argue that their business is private and that they cannot be considered part of the state or the state's police system. Therefore, they say, the 14th Amendment does not apply to them, and they need no due process.

Weisz contends, on the other hand, that repossession is governed by state law to such a degree that the private character of the conduct cannot be separated from its public nature. He is mainly concerned with the issue of legality of repossessions as such, but most attorneys in the consumer and constitutional law fields worry most about the manner in which repossessions are carried out more than their legality.

"They come in the middle of the night. They'll take your car whether it's locked or not. They don't care whether it's on the street or on your property. Some don't even care whether it's in a locked garage," says one lawyer with a legal-aid group. "They'll take it any way they can."

The buyer has little legal ground on which to avert a repossession, even if the question of default is disputable. Any legal determination as to who is entitled to the car, the debtor or the creditor, is made after the fact. First they repossess. Then it's up to you to prove that they had no right to do so. Lawyers agree that most repossessions are valid. The buyer doesn't make his payments, so the creditor takes back his car.

"The problem is," complains one attorney, "that too many repossessors think the end justifies the means."

The law puts only one basic limitation on the process of automobile repossessions—they must be accomplished without a breach of the peace. Breach of peace has been defined in one California court decision as "acts causing public turbulence, acts of violence generally, and acts and words likely to produce violence in others."

In fact, all you have to do is raise a big enough ruckus when the repossessors come and you have established a breach of peace on their part. In the end, it may well boil down to one thing, however—who is bigger, you or the repossessor.

The risk of violence is always present, and sometimes it has gone to ugly and tragic extremes. In 1974, a Los Angeles man who spotted his car being towed off by a repossessor gave chase and fired five revolver shots at the tow truck. The last shot hit its intended target and killed the driver.

The breach of peace clause has been augmented by a number of court decisions further defining and clarifying the rights of the creditor and debtor; but, it appears there are still many more questions than answers. For instance:

Can the repossessor seize a locked car?
Can he take it from your yard or driveway?
Can he take it from your garage?
Can he open a gate or pick a lock to get at it?

None of these questions has been answered so definitively as to be beyond challenge. Courts have ruled either way. This, of course, isn't much comfort to anyone who gets behind on his car payments and is sweating out the prospect of having it repossessed. A broad, general outline on where repossessions may take place, according to several lawyers, could run something like this.

Street or public parking lot. If the car is not locked, it can without question be legally repossessed. If it is locked, the citizen may have a case. He could argue that securing a car by locking it is an implied revocation of consent to repossession. (The consent to repossession is usually contained in a clause of the sales contract. It requires the buyer to waive his right to the car if he defaults on the payments.)
Yard or driveway. The creditor may repossess if he can do it in a peaceful manner. He is considered to have a consensual privilege to enter the debtor's land for purposes of repossession, but it can be argued that the debtor may withdraw this right when repossession is attempted. "In effect," offered one attorney, "the repossessor can

take your car from your land as long as you aren't there to say no to him."

Garage. One court has ruled that the creditor is not permitted to enter a locked or closed garage without express consent of the debtor at the time of repossession. On the other hand, it could be argued that opening a garage door, or even picking a lock, does not constitute breach of peace. It could further be argued that trespass laws do not apply because the buyer waived his right to sue for trespass when he signed the contract and consented to repossession.

Any and all of these questions are moot unless they are raised in court, and that doesn't happen too often. People just don't go running out to hire a lawyer when their cars are repossessed. Most people in this predicament can't afford an attorney, or don't believe they can. But the Legal Aid Society can offer help and legal counsel in this area, too. Most debtors either pay, whether they feel they should or not, or they default. Total default can be doubly costly.

The creditor can resell the car and, if the proceeds don't cover the debt, get a deficiency judgment against the buyer for the balance. The buyer not only loses the car but also still owes money. Many consumer attorneys, like Weisz, feel the law surrounding deficiency judgments is inadequate. The law requires only that the creditor sell the car in a commercially reasonable manner. It says nothing about a commercially reasonable *price.* That means the creditor could conceivably seize a $1000 car to satisfy a $750 debt, sell the car for $500, and sue you for the difference of $250.

You do have legal recourse, however. You too can sue. The trouble is, though, that most people who have had a car repossessed can't usually afford an attorney and may not even qualify for help from a legal-aid group. That's what creditors count on. But legal-aid attorneys in some cities are beginning to turn the tables a little.

Consumer defender Ken Roye says he has handled dozens of repossession cases and won most of them. But although that may satisfy the few individuals concerned, he says, it's almost an exercise in futility.

"For every case that's contested, there are a hundred that aren't. The dealers and the lenders couldn't care less if they lose 15 or 20 cases a year to consumer lawyers. They know there aren't too many of us."

But it's still worth a fight if you think you're right.

Appendix 1

Where to Write for Help

Organizations

American Bar Association
Consumer Affairs Committee
1255 Cook Avenue
Cleveland, Ohio 44107

Council of Better Business Bureaus, Inc.
1150 17th Street, N.W.
Washington, D.C. 20036

Independent Garage Owners of America
3261 West Fullerton Street
Chicago, Illinois 60605

National Automobile Dealers Association
2000 K Street, N.W.
Washington, D.C. 20006

National Consumer Groups

Ralph Nader
Center for Auto Safety
800 National Press Building
Washington, D.C. 20004

Consumer Federation of America
1012 14th Street, N.W.
Washington, D.C. 20005

Consumers Union of U.S., Inc.
256 Washington Street
Mount Vernon, New York 10550

Federal Agencies

Federal Trade Commission
Bureau of Consumer Protection
Pennsylvania Avenue at 6th Street, N.W.
Washington, D.C. 20580

National Highway Traffic Safety Administration
Defects Investigation
400 7th Street, S.W.
Washington, D.C. 20591

Senator Philip Hart
Senate Subcommittee on Antitrust and Monopoly
414 Old Senate Office Building
Washington, D.C. 20510

White House Office of Consumer Affairs
New Executive Office Building
Washington, D.C. 20506

Local Agencies and Consumer Groups Listed by State

ALABAMA
Alabama Consumers Association
P.O. Box 1372
Birmingham 35201

Attorney General of Alabama
State Administration Building
Montgomery 36104

ALASKA
Alaska Consumer Council
833 13th Street West
Anchorage 99501

Attorney General of Alaska
Pouch "K"
State Capitol
Juneau 99801

ARIZONA
Director, Division of Consumer Fraud
Office of Attorney General
159 State Capitol Building
Phoenix 85007

ARKANSAS
Attorney General
Consumer Protection Division
Justice Building
Little Rock 72201

CALIFORNIA
American Consumers Council
9720 Wilshire Boulevard
Suite 203
Beverly Hills 90212

Association of California Consumers
3030 Bridgeway Building
Sausalito 94965

Attorney General
Consumer Fraud Section
State Office Building, Room 600
Los Angeles 90012

Bay Area Consumer Protection Committee
c/o Department of Justice
6000 State Building
San Francisco 94102

The Citizen Advocate Office
Byron Bloch, Director
P.O. Box 49867
West Los Angeles 90049

Citizens for Consumer Action
4230 De Costa Avenue
Sacramento 95821

Consumer Alliance
P.O. Box 11773
Palo Alto 94306

Consumer Protection Committee of the City of Los Angeles
City Hall, Room 303
Los Angeles 90013

Bureau of Automotive Repair
Department of Consumer Affairs
1020 N Street
Sacramento 95814

Santa Clara County Department of Consumer Affairs
409 Mathew Street
Santa Clara 95050

Division of Consumer Affairs
Ventura County
608 El Rio Drive
Oxnard 93030

Los Angeles Consumer Protection Committee
11000 Wilshire Boulevard
Los Angeles 90024

COLORADO
Attorney General, Colorado Office of Consumer Affairs
Department of Law
503 Farmers Union Building
1575 Sherman Street
Denver 80203

Colorado Consumers Association, Inc.
P.O. Box 989
Boulder 80302

Colorado League of Consumer Protection
8230 West 16th Place
Lakewood 80215

CONNECTICUT
Attorney General of Connecticut
Capitol Annex
30 Trinity Place
Hartford 06115

Connecticut Citizen Action Group
57 Farmington Avenue
Hartford 06105

Connecticut Consumer Association, Inc.
One Lafayette Circle
Bridgeport 06603

Commissioner
Department of Consumer Protection
State Office Building
Hartford 06115

DELAWARE
Attorney General of Delaware
Consumer Protection Division
1206 King Street
Wilmington 19801

Department of Consumer Affairs
Old State House
Dover 19901

Director
Division of Consumer Affairs
704 Delaware Avenue
Wilmington 19801

DISTRICT OF COLUMBIA
City Hall Complaint Center
Office of Community Services
14th and E Streets, N.W.
Washington, D.C. 20004

Consumer Association of the District of Columbia
328 D Street, N.E.
Washington, D.C. 20002

D.C. Citywide Consumer Council
745 50th Street, N.E.
Washington, D.C. 20019

George Washington University Consumer Protection Center
Room 3 Harlan-Brewer House
714 21st Street, N.W.
Washington, D.C. 20006

Neighborhood Consumer Information Center
Howard University
3005 Georgia Avenue
Washington, D.C. 20001

Consumer Protection Branch, United Planning Organization
1344 Maryland Avenue, N.E.
Washington, D.C. 20002

U.S. Attorney's Office
Consumer Fraud Unit
U.S. Courthouse, Constitution and John Marshall Place
Washington, D.C. 20001

FLORIDA
American Consumer Association
P.O. Box 24141
Fort Lauderdale 33307

Attorney General of Florida
The Capitol
Tallahassee 32304

Division of Consumer Affairs
City of Jacksonville
Department of Public Safety
220 East Bay Street
Jacksonville 32202

Director of Consumer Affairs, City of St. Petersburg
264 First Avenue, N.
St. Petersburg 33701

Consumer Protection Division, Dade County
1351 Northwest 12th Street
Miami 33125

Consumers Affairs Council
208 Southeast 3rd Avenue
Fort Lauderdale 33312

Director of Consumer Services, Department of Agriculture
   and Consumer Services
The Capitol
Tallahassee 32304

Florida Consumers Association, Inc.
Box 3552
Tallahassee 32303

GEORGIA
Attorney General
132 State Judicial Building
Atlanta 30334

Georgia Consumer Council
Box 311
Morris Brown College
Atlanta 30314

Georgia Consumer Services Program
15 Peachtree Street, Room 909
Atlanta 30303

HAWAII
Attorney General of Hawaii
Honolulu 96813

Director of Consumer Protection
Office of the Governor
P.O. Box 3767
Honolulu 96811

IDAHO
Attorney General
Consumer Protection Division
State Capitol
Boise 83702

ILLINOIS
Attorney General of Illinois,
    Consumer Fraud Section
134 North LaSalle Street
Room 204
Chicago 60602

Chicago Consumer Protection Committee
Room 486
U.S. Courthouse and Federal Building
219 South Dearborn Street
Chicago 60604

Chicago Department of Consumer Sales, City Hall
121 North LaSalle Street
Chicago 60602

Cook County Consumer Fraud Bureau
160 North LaSalle Street
Chicago 60601

Illinois Citizens for Automobile Safety
5445 Hyde Park Boulevard
Chicago 60615

Illinois Federation of Consumers
53 West Jackson Boulevard
Chicago 60604

Students for Consumer Protection
P.O. Box 443
Rockford 61105

INDIANA
Attorney General of Indiana
Office of Consumer Protection
219 State House
Indianapolis 46204

Consumer Advisory Council
c/o Indiana Department of Commerce
336 State House
Indianapolis 46204

Consumers Association of Indiana, Inc.
910 North Delaware Street
Indianapolis 46202

IOWA
Attorney General of Iowa
Consumer Protection Division
20 East 13th Court
Des Moines 50319

Iowa Consumers League
P.O. Box 1076
Des Moines 50311

KANSAS
Consumer Frauds Division
Office of Attorney General
The Capitol
Topeka 66612

Consumer Protection Division
Sedgwick County Courthouse
Wichita 67203

Consumer United Program
8410 West Highway 54
Wichita 67209

Kansas City Consumer Association
7720 West 61st Street
Shawnee Mission 66202

KENTUCKY
Attorney General of Kentucky
Consumer Protection Division
State Capitol
Frankfort 40601

Chairman, Citizens' Commission for Consumer Protection
State Capitol
Frankfort 40601

Consumer Association of Kentucky, Inc.
4515 Bishop Lane
Louisville 40218

Division of Consumer Affairs
City of Louisville
Metropolitan Sewer District Building
Louisville 40202

LOUISIANA
Attorney General
State Capitol
Baton Rouge 70804

Louisiana Consumers' League
P.O. Box 1332
Baton Rouge 70821

New Orleans Consumer Protection Committee
1000 Masonic Temple Building
333 St. Charles Street
New Orleans 70130

MAINE
Attorney General's Office
Consumer Protection Division
State House
Augusta 04330

MARYLAND
Attorney General, Consumer Protection Division
One Charles Center
Baltimore 21201

Executive Secretary
Consumer Protection Commission
Prince Georges County Courthouse
Upper Marlboro 20870

Maryland Auto Safety Research Center
37 Reckford Armory
University of Maryland
College Park 20740

Maryland Consumers Association, Inc.
P.O. Box 143
Annapolis 21404

Montgomery County Consumer Protection Office
24 South Perry Street
Rockville 20850

MASSACHUSETTS
Boston Consumers' Council
218 Weld Avenue
West Roxbury 02119

Boston Metropolitan Consumer Protection Committee
c/o Federal Trade Commission, J. F. Kennedy Federal Building
Government Center
Boston 02203

Consumer Protection Division
Department of the Attorney General, State House
Boston 02133

Massachusetts Consumer Association
27 School Street
Boston 02108

Massachusetts Consumers' Council
State Office Building
100 Cambridge Street
Boston 02202

MICHIGAN

Attorney General
Consumer Protection Division
The Capitol
Lansing 48903

Detroit Consumer Protection Committee
333 Mt. Elliott Avenue
Detroit 48207

Interagency Consumer Commission
Office of the Mayor, City Hall
Detroit 48226

Chairman
Michigan Consumer Council
525 Hollister Building
Lansing 48933

Special Assistant to the Governor for Consumer Affairs
1033 South Washington Street
Lansing 48910

MINNESOTA

Attorney General
Consumer Division
102 State Capitol
St. Paul 55101

Complaints, Inc.
Michael Kane
3343 East Calhoun
Minneapolis 55408

Office of Consumer Services
Department of Commerce
Room 230, State Office Building
St. Paul 55101

Minnesota Consumers League
P.O. Box 3063
St. Paul 55101

MISSISSIPPI
Attorney General
Consumer Protection Division
State Capitol
Jackson 39201

Consumer Protection Division
Department of Agriculture and Commerce
Jackson 39205

Mississippi Consumer Association
1601 Terrace Road
Cleveland 38732

MISSOURI
Citizens Consumer Advisory Committee
7701 Forsyth Boulevard
Clayton 63104

Executive Director
Office of Consumer Affairs
Department of Welfare
St. Louis 63103

Kansas City Consumer Association
940 South Woodland Drive
Kansas City 64118

Missouri Association of Consumers
P.O. Box 514
Columbia 65201

Consumer Protection Division
Office of the Attorney General
Supreme Court Building
Jefferson 65101

St. Louis Consumer Federation
6321 Darlow Drive
St. Louis 63123

MONTANA
Administrative Assistant to the Governor
The Capitol
Helena 59601

Montana Consumer Affairs Council
301 West Lawrence
Helena 59601

NEBRASKA
Attorney General
State Capitol
Lincoln 68509

NEVADA
Attorney General
Supreme Court Building
Carson City 89701

NEW HAMPSHIRE
Attorney General of New Hampshire
State House Annex
Concord 03301

Chairman, New Hampshire Consumer Council
8 Pepperidge Drive
Manchester 03103

NEW JERSEY
Attorney General of New Jersey
State House Annex
Trenton 08625

Camden County Office of Consumer Affairs
Commerce Building #1 Broadway
Camden 08101

Consumers League of New Jersey
20 Church Street
Montclair 07042

Executive Director
Office of Consumer Protection
Department of Law and Public Safety
1100 Raymond Boulevard
Newark 07102

NEW MEXICO
Albuquerque Consumers Association
4844 Southern Avenue, S.E.
Albuquerque 87108

Director, Consumer Protection Division
Attorney General's Office
Supreme Court Building, Box 2246
Santa Fe 87501

NEW YORK
Attorney General
The Capitol
Albany 12225

Consumer Protection Board
380 Madison Avenue
New York 10017

Consumer Affairs
City of Long Beach
City Hall
Long Beach 11561

Metropolitan New York Consumer Council
1710 Broadway
New York 10019

Commissioner
Office of Consumer Affairs
Nassau County
160 Old Country Road
Mineola 11501

Bess Myerson Grant, Commissioner
City of New York Department of Consumer Affairs
80 Lafayette Street
New York 10013

Consumer Frauds and Protection Bureau
Office of Attorney General
80 Centre Street
New York 10013

Office of Consumer Affairs
County of Orange
Goshen 10924

Consumer Assembly of Greater New York, Inc.
c/o United Housing Foundation
465 Grand Street
New York 10002

Consumer Council of Monroe County
P.O. Box 3209, Federal Station
Rochester 14614

NORTH CAROLINA
Attorney General
Department of Justice Building
Consumer Protection Division
P.O. Box 629
Raleigh 27602

North Carolina Consumers Council
108 East Jefferson Street
Monroe 28110

NORTH DAKOTA
Attorney General
Consumer Fraud Division, State Capitol
Bismarck 58501

OHIO
Chief, Consumer Frauds and Crimes Section
Attorney General's Office
State House Annex
Columbus 43215

Auto Safety Research Center—Cleveland
Room 102, Case Main
10900 Euclid Avenue
Cleveland 44106

City Sealer of Weights and Measures
City Hall
Columbus 43215

Consumer Conference of Greater Cincinnati
318 Terrace Avenue
Cincinnati 44114

Consumers League of Ohio
940 Engineers Building
Cleveland 45402

Cleveland Consumer Protection Association
Mall Building
118 St. Clair Avenue
Cleveland 45402

Ohio Consumers Association
P.O. Box 1559
Columbus 43216

OKLAHOMA
Attorney General
112 State Capitol
Oklahoma City 73105

Consumers Council of Oklahoma
240 East Apache
Tulsa 74107

Department of Consumer Affairs
Lincoln Office Plaza, Suite 74
4545 Lincoln Boulevard
Oklahoma City 73105

OREGON
Assistant to the Governor for Consumer Services
State Capitol Building
Salem 97301

Attorney General
Consumer Protection
322 State Office Building
Salem 97310

Metropolitan Consumer Protection Agency
Multnomah County
Court House
Portland 97204

Oregon Consumer League
919 Northwest 19th Avenue
Portland 97232

PENNSYLVANIA
Allegheny County
Bureau of Consumer Protection
209 Jones Law Building Annex
Pittsburgh 15212

Alliance for Consumer Protection
5700 Bunkerhill Street #1002
Pittsburgh 15206

Consumers Education and Protective Association
6048 Ogontz Avenue
Philadelphia 19141

Model Cities Community
Consumer Protection Program
1521 West Girard Avenue
Philadelphia 19130

National Student Consumer Protection Council
c/o Professor A. S. Butkys
Villanova University
Villanova 19085

Director
Bureau of Consumer Protection
Pennsylvania Department of Justice
2 North Market Square
Harrisburg 17101

Pennsylvania League for Consumer Protection
P.O. Box 948
Harrisburg 17108

Consumer Services
City of Philadelphia
City Hall, Room 210
Philadelphia 19106

Philadelphia Consumer Protection Committee
53 Long Lane
Upper Darby 19082

RHODE ISLAND
Attorney General
Consumer Affairs Section
Providence County Court House
Providence 02903

Executive Director
Rhode Island Consumer Council
365 Broadway
Providence 02902

Rhode Island Consumers' League
131 Washington Street
Providence 02903

SOUTH CAROLINA
Attorney General
Hampton Office Building
Columbia 29201

SOUTH DAKOTA
Attorney General
Office of Consumer Affairs
The Capitol
Pierre 57501

South Dakota Consumers League
Sturgis 50039

TENNESSEE
Executive Director
Advisory Commission on Consumer Protection
Nashville 37219

Attorney General
Supreme Court Building
Nashville 37219

Tennessee Consumer Alliance
P.O. Box 12352, Acklen Station
Nashville 37212

TEXAS
Attorney General
Anti-Trust & Consumer Protection Division
Supreme Court Building
Austin 78711

Commissioner of Consumer Credit
1011 San Jacinto
P.O. Box 2107
Austin 78767

Texas Consumer Association
505 North Ervoy Building
Suite 99
Dallas 75201

UTAH
Administrator of Consumer Credit
403 State Capitol
Salt Lake City 84114

Attorney General
Consumer Protection Section
236 Capitol Building
Salt Lake City 84114

League of Utah Consumers
c/o Utah Credit Union League
1706 Major Street
Salt Lake City 84115

VERMONT
Attorney General, Consumer Protection Bureau
94 Church Street
Burlington 05401

Vermont Consumers' Association
72 Lakewood Parkway
Burlington 05401

VIRGINIA
Arlington County Consumer
Protection Office
2049 North 15th Street
Arlington 22201

Attorney General
Supreme Court, Library Building
Richmond 23219

Fairfax County Consumer Protection Commission
4100 Chain Bridge Road
Fairfax 22030

Special Assistant to the
    Governor for Consumer Affairs
Office of the Governor
Richmond 23219

Virginia Beach Consumer Protection Officer
Bureau of Consumer Protection
City Hall
Virginia Beach 23456

Virginia Citizens Consumer Council
P.O. Box 3103
Alexandria 22303

Office of Consumer Affairs
Virginia Department of Agriculture and Commerce
8th Street Office Building
Richmond 23219

WASHINGTON
Attorney General
Consumer Protection Division
1266 Dexter Horton Building
Seattle 98104

Washington Committee on Consumer Interests
2700 First Avenue
Seattle 98121

WEST VIRGINIA
Attorney General
State Capitol
Charleston 25305

Consumer Protection Division
West Virginia Department of Labor
1900 Washington Street East
Charleston 25305

West Virginia Consumer Association
410 12th Avenue
Huntington 25701

WISCONSIN
Attorney General
Office of Consumer Protection
The Capitol
Madison 53702

Center for Consumer Affairs
University of Wisconsin, Milwaukee
600 West Kilbourn Avenue
Milwaukee 53203

Madison Consumer League
117 West Main Street
Madison 53703

Wisconsin Consumers League
P.O. Box 1531
Madison 53701

WYOMING
Attorney General
120 Capitol Building
Cheyenne 82001

Administrator
Consumer Credit Code
State Supreme Court Building
Cheyenne 82001

PUERTO RICO
Attorney General
P.O. Box 192
San Juan 00902

Consumer Services Administration
P.O. Box 13934
Santurce 00908

VIRGIN ISLANDS
Public Services Commission
Charlotte Amalie
St. Thomas 00801

CANADA
L. P. Edmonston, President
Automobile Protection Association
P.O. Box 117, Station E
Montreal 151, Quebec

Consumers Association of Canada
100 Gloucester Street
Ottawa 4, Ontario

Department of Consumer and Corporate Affairs
219 Laurier Avenue West
Ottawa Ontario, KIA OC9

Appendix 2

An Automotive Dictionary

Accelerator: The "gas pedal" which, when depressed, opens the throttle valve on the carburetor and feeds a mixture of air and fuel to the engine's cylinders.

Accelerator linkage: The levers that connect the pedal to the carburetor. Proper adjustment of these components is important in making sure the accelerator does not stick open or respond sluggishly.

Additives: Lubricants (usually syrupy) added to the engine oil for increased protection against friction, heat, and wear. There is considerable controversy and disagreement among automotive experts as to the value of these widely advertised products. Regular oil changes and use of the proper grade of oil makes the use of additives optional.

Alternator: Used on most modern cars in place of the generator. Its biggest advantage over the generator is that it produces current at lower rpm, even when the engine is only idling.

Ammeter: This instrument measures the amount of electricity in amperes being charged into or discharged from your car's battery. Most cars today, however, employ "idiot lights" which are supposed to flash a red signal if something goes wrong. The gauge is much superior as a means of detecting trouble. The lights are merely money savers for auto makers.

Ampere: A measured unit of electrical current sent by one volt through a basic resistance unit called an ohm.

Antifreeze: This can be any liquid used in the car's cooling system which has a lower freezing point than water. It protects the cooling system and the engine's interior components from rust and corrosion, and from freezing when the air temperature drops below the freezing point of 32 degrees Fahrenheit.

Anti-knock: A chemical substance added to the fuel to eliminate or reduce the rattling noise caused by combustion ignition coming a little too early.

Armature: That part of the generator or electric motor which revolves and carries the electrical current.

Axle: The rods or shafts on which the car's wheels spin.

Ball joints: A ball and socket device on which the front wheels swivel for steering purposes.

Bands: Metal belts inside the automatic transmission that transmit power when they tighten.

Battery: A device which uses chemical means to store electrical energy and supply it when you turn the ignition key to start your car.

Bleeding the brakes: A term used to describe clearing the hydraulic system of unwanted air pockets.

Block: The main casting or body of the engine which houses most of the working parts (cylinders, pistons, crankshaft, etc.).

Blow-by: Oily blue smoke coming out of the engine when the oil filler cap is removed. This is the first sign that a worn-out engine needs new piston rings.

Blow out: The bursting of a tire.

Bore: This has nothing whatsoever to do with how interesting your car is. These are holes in the engine block which house the pistons that drive the crankshaft. The diameter of these holes is called the bore.

Brake drums: These are the flat, curved insides of a car's brakes against which the brake shoes rub.

Brake fluid: When you depress the brake pedal inside the car, a liquid substance called brake fluid builds up pressure within the hydraulic system and transmits the force that activates the brakes.

Brake linings: Fibrous covers on the brake shoes which reduce wear and help absorb heat created by friction generated by the shoes' rubbing against the drums.

Brake shoes: When the brakes are activated, the shoes, which are two semicircular metal blocks, press outward against the circular inside surfaces of the brake drums, thus slowing the wheels and the vehicle.

Cam or camshaft: One of the most important components of an engine. The cam is a shaft that operates the valves. It can be compared in both its function and importance to the human heart.

Car: If you don't know what this is, why did you read the book? Congratulations, nevertheless!

Carburetor: A device, usually located on top of the engine, which mixes the correct proportions of air and fuel and then feeds it into the engine cylinders.

Charge: Not to be confused with installment buying. A method of replenishing the electrical energy stored in your car's battery. There is a similarity, isn't there!

Chassis: The lower components of a car, including the frame, wheels, engine, transmission, axles, and differential.

Choke: A small valve connected to the carburetor which adjusts the mixture of air and fuel. It helps to get the engine running when it's cold.

Clutch: A device which permits the transmission to pick up the power from the engine slowly until the gears are turning at the same speed as the engine. Without the coordinating effort of the clutch, the teeth of the transmission gears would be stripped away or the drive shaft would snap.

Coil: An electrical component which steps up the necessary voltage for the spark plugs.

Condenser: A device used for receiving and momentarily storing electrical current. It is usually found inside the distributor cap.

Connecting rods: The up-and-down motion of the pistons is transmitted to the crankshaft via these rods.

Crankcase: A metal pan or casing that covers the bottom of the engine and contains the oil. It is often referred to as the oil pan.

Crankshaft: The main engine shaft which converts the up-and-down motion of the pistons into spinning motion for drive power.

Cubic inches: Engine sizes are usually described in terms of cubic inches, which is merely the number of cubic inches of space that the pistons displace in each cylinder multiplied by the number of cylinders. It has nothing to do with "horsepower." A 400-cubic-inch V8 engine means there are 50 cubic inches in each cylinder. We'll explain horsepower later. Most imported cars are measured by the metric system of liters. One liter is roughly equivalent to 61 cubic inches. Therefore a 5-liter engine would be approximately 305ci.

Cylinders: Holes bored into the engine block where pistons fit and combustion takes place are called cylinders. The brake system also has a master cylinder, which contains the bulk of brake fluid. This is the most important cylinder in the car as far as you're concerned, and the fluid level should be checked at least once a month. Service-station attendants can handle the job.

Differential: These are the gears that transmit the spinning motion or torque of the drive shaft to the drive axle, which is at the rear of most cars.

Disc brakes: Probably the most efficient brake system now used. Instead of the drum and shoe setup, disc brakes consist of large metal discs or plates called rotors mounted on the axle behind the wheel. When the brakes are activated these discs are squeezed between small fibrous shoes in what are called calipers. The result is smoother and quicker stopping with less brake fade than with the drum variety.

Distributor: Each cylinder in your car's engine requires combustion in a definite sequence. The distributor, with help from the coil, condenser, and points, sends the right amount of electricity at the right time to the spark plugs in each cylinder.

Drive shaft: The long spinning shaft resembling a large water pipe that connects the transmission with the drive axle underneath your car. If it breaks, which doesn't happen often, your car will be rendered immobile.

Exhaust manifold: These are the pipe-like castings on the engine that carry the exhaust gases from the cylinders to the exhaust pipe and out into the air we breathe.

Fog: In auto-repair circles this is not to be confused with the misty substance in the sky which sometimes settles near the ground and limits visibility. But the effects are indeed similar. Around repair shops this term is used to describe taking a paint spray gun and lightly covering up a fault in the paint job of a customer's car, i.e., "fogging the paint," or "fog-in the paint."

Gasket: A soft fibrous material placed between two metal surfaces to prevent liquids and gases from leaking.

Gears: These are wheels with teeth on the outer edges, allowing them to interlock and pass the motion of one on to another.

Generator: This is a device that transforms mechanical energy into electricity. On automobiles the generator takes over once the engine is running, and it then recharges the battery.

Governor: In the automotive industry this device controls the top speed of a vehicle by regulating the amount of air/fuel mixture entering the carburetor.

Horsepower: One of the most misunderstood and meaningless terms in the automotive world. The most important thing to remember is that large horsepower usually means poor gas mileage. It does not necessarily mean high performance. Many of the fastest cars in the world, such as Formula 1 Grand Prix racers, have very small engines and low horsepower. But for you sticklers who want a specific answer, horsepower is defined as a foot-pound/second unit of power, equivalent to 550 foot-pounds per second.

Hydraulic: A system operated by the applied pressure of a liquid, as in hydraulic brakes.

Ignition: An intricate system of electrical devices that distributes the correct amount of current to the spark plugs to ignite the air/fuel mixture in the cylinders. You activate this system by turning the ignition key.

Intake manifold: A metal passageway through which the air/fuel mixture passes from the carburetor into the cylinders.

Miss: An uneven firing of the cylinders caused by improper ignition or more serious internal malfunctions such as burned valves or rings.

Muffler: A metal box usually stuffed with asbestos and fiberglass to deaden the sound of the engine.

Octane: Most car owners believe high octane denotes a more powerful gasoline. Wrong, wrong, wrong. Octane is a paraffin hydrocarbon added to almost all gasolines in order to cut down the knock or pinging in some high-compression engines. Octane rating merely measures the ability of a gasoline to resist knocking, with higher octane gasolines more resistant. High-compression engines require high-octane gasoline, usually referred to as *premium*. The term *ethyl* refers to tetraethyl lead, a poisonous compound also added to gasoline to prevent knock. Neither compound increases power. Since 1975 most cars require lead-free gasoline to provide emission control and reduce air pollution.

PCV (Positive Crankcase Ventilation) valve: This is a valve (naturally) that regulates the flow of some exhaust gases back into the combustion chambers instead of polluting the atmosphere.

Piston: These are short plunger-like cylinders fitted inside the engine cylinders. They move up and down as a result of the burning of the air/fuel mixture ignited by the spark plugs.

Piston rings: These are fitted into small grooves on each piston to insure the pistons fit tightly against the cylinder walls.

Points: Located under the distributor cap, points serve as a switch to control electrical spark production.

Radiator: This is a pressurized container made up basically of a series of thin tubes called the *core*. Its main purpose is to store and cool the water as it circulates through the engine.

Shock absorber: Despite the name, shock absorbers do not absorb the shock of running over bumps. The springs do that. These hydraulic tubes keep the car from continuing to bounce and bounce and bounce long after the springs have taken the shock out of hitting a bump. That's why you can tell a car needs new shocks if it rocks and bounces along like an obese baby buggy riding on a washboard. Can you really picture that?

Solenoid: An electrical switch which activates the starter motor when the ignition is turned on.

Spark plugs: Electrical conductors screwed into the tops of the cylinders to transmit spark and ignite the air/fuel mixture.

Starter motor: An electric motor that spins the engine to get it started.

Stroke: You may have heard the expression "bore and stroke." Turn back a few pages if you don't remember what bore is. Stroke simply describes the distance a piston travels either moving up or down in the cylinder.

Suspension: This describes the system of springs and shocks under the car that keeps the ride smooth, stable, and comfortable. High performance and racing cars sacrifice some of that spongy comfort in exchange for better cornering and handling in general.

Thermostat: This small and inexpensive item on your car is built into the cooling system to help stabilize the temperature of the circulating water or coolant.

Tie rods: These connect the front wheels with the steering mechanism. They should be checked every time your car is serviced.

Torque: A much used and misunderstood term, torque is a measurement of turning or twisting force.

Torque converter: An important component of automatic transmissions which can both transmit torque and multiply it.

Torsion bar: Metal rods used instead of springs in the suspension of some cars.

Transmission: The box of gears behind the engine (except in some rear- or mid-engine cars) which transmits power from the engine to the wheels.

Universal joints or U-joints: These are couplings which permit a degree of flexing in the drive shaft.

Valves: As the name implies, these are little stoppers at the top of each cylinder that open and close to let the air/fuel mixture in and the exhaust out.

Water pump: The device responsible for circulating engine coolant.

Index

AAMCO, 71-72
Advertising, misleading, 71-72
Air cleaner, 99
Air conditioners, 140
Air-cooled engines, 105
Air horn, 98
Alternator, 105, 107, 108
   frauds involving, 39
American Automobile Association
   (AAA), 80
   road service program of, 43
Antifreeze coolant, 104, 129, 130
Assembly line, automobile, 10-11
Auto accessory shops, 73

Balancing tires, 136
Ball joints, 41
Batteries, 105, 107-108, 130-131, 138
   frauds involving, 38-39
Better Business Bureau, 146
B. F. Goodrich, 73
Body of automobile, 85-87, 126
Brake system, 41, 81, 120-124, 132-134
Breaker points, 107, 108, 136
Butterfly, 99

Caliper, 121-123
Camshaft, 94, 98, 107
Carburetor, 98, 99, 112
Center link, 118-120
Certification programs for mechanics, 33-34
Charging system, 105-110, 130-131

Chassis, 85, 87, 126
Choke, 99, 132
Circuits, 107
Clutch, 110
Combustion chamber, 92
Condenser, 107, 136
Connecting rod, 88, 90, 92
Coolant, 104, 129, 130
Cooling system, 101-105, 129-130
Cooperative Auto Shop of San Francisco,
   Inc., 63-65
Core, 101
Court cases, 153-154
   small claims, 151-152
Crankcase, 92, 93
Crankshaft, 88, 90, 92, 94
Cylinder block, 92
Cylinder head, 92

Dealer preparation, 11-12, 52, 54
Dealerships, new-car, 13, 14, 65-69,
   146-147
   fraudulent practices of, 38
   selection of, 53
Diagnostic centers, 79-82
Differential, 87, 110, 115
Disc brakes, 121-123
Distributor, 78, 107, 108, 110, 131
Drive line, 87, 110
Drum brakes, 121
Dual overhead cam engines, 94
Dynamometer, 81

Electrical system, 105-110, 130-131
Engine, 87, 88-94, 128-129
Estimates for repairs, 26, 28-30, 42
Exhaust manifold, 99, 140
Exhaust pipe, 99
Exhaust system, maintenance of, 131-132

Factory trained mechanic, 31, 32, 68
Fan belt, 101
Federal law, warranties and, 58-59, 61
Federal regulations, model updating and, 46-47
Federal Trade Commission (FTC), 71-72, 146
Filters
  air, 131-132, 136
  fuel, 98, 131, 136
  oil, 105, 128
Firestone, 73
Flat rates, 13, 14, 28, 67-68, 76
Float bowl, 98-99
Fluid coupling, 111
Flywheel, 88, 108, 110, 112
Foreign cars, 10
Frame, 87
Frauds, automotive repair
  examples of, 36-47
  laws and, 15-16, 20-21
  legal defenses, 150-157
Front-end alignment problems, 55, 135-136
Fuel line, 94, 98
Fuel pump, 94, 98
Fuel system, maintenance of, 131-132
Fuel tank, 94, 98

"Garage station," 74
Gaskets, 93, 128
Gasoline, 88
Gasoline mileage, 131, 132, 139-141
Gears, 111, 115
General Automobile Mechanic (GAM), 33
General Tire, 73
Generator, 39, 105
Goodyear, 73
Guarantees
  garage "50-50," 57
  laws and, 57-61
  parts, 57
  value of new-car. See Warranty, new-car

Heater, 104
Horizontal opposed arrangement of cylinders, 92

Hydraulic brakes, 120, 121, 124
Hydraulic valve lifter, 94

Idler arm, 118, 120
Ignition coil, 107
Ignition system, 107
Independent garages, 75-79, 147-148
Independent Garage Owners of America, 33, 148
In-line arrangement of cylinders, 92
Insulation, 87
Intake manifold, 98

Kelley Blue Book, 46

Labor rates, 75, 76
Laws
  enforcement of, 15-16, 20-21
  guarantees and, 57-61
  model updating and, 44-47
  See also Legal defenses
Leaks, water, 56
Legal Aid Society, 154, 157
Legal defenses, 150-157
Letter, complaint, 148-150
Lien, mechanic's, 26-29
Lubrication, 56, 93, 105, 115, 129

Magnuson-Moss Warranty-FTC
  Improvements Act, 58, 61
Main discharge nozzle, 98-99
Maintenance, regular, 125-138
Maintenance programs, 56-57, 69
Mass merchandisers, 69-73
Mechanical tappets, 94
Mechanic's lien, 26-29
Mechanics
  certification of, 33-34
  incompetence of, 23-26
  number of, 32
  qualifications of, 15, 33
  service station, 73-74
  training of, 31-33
Midas, 71-72
Model year updating, 43-47
Mufflers, 99-101

National Automobile Dealers Association
  (NADA), 14, 33, 67
National Automotive Technicians
  Certification Board (NATCB), 33
National Institute for Automotive Service
  Excellence (NIASE), 81

Obsolescence, planned, 10
Office of Consumer Affairs, 16
Oil
    change, 56, 105, 128
    drippings under car, 93, 128
    filter, 105, 128
    grades, 105, 129
    level, 115
Overhead cam engines, 94
Overheating, 104, 130

Painting rebuilt parts, 42-43
Parts
    brand name, 68
    rebuilt, 42-43
    repairing, 76
    replacing, 68, 70, 77
PCV system, maintenance of, 131
Piston, 88
Piston pin, 88
Piston rings, 93
Pitman arm, 118, 120
Ports, 99
Power train, 87, 110-115
Push rod, 94, 120

Radiator, 101, 104, 129
Rear axle, 87, 110, 115
Repairs, unauthorized, 28
Repossessions, fighting, 154-157
Resistor, 107, 108
Road tests, 12, 52, 53, 55-56
Rocker arms, 93

Sabotaging cars, 38-39
Safety of cars, 11
Service stations, 73-75, 146
Shock absorbers, 117-118, 135
    checking, 40, 117-118
"Short-sticking," 38
Small claims court, 151-152
Solenoid switch, 77, 108
Spark plugs, 88, 90, 107, 108, 110, 131,
    136
Specialization in repair work, 68
Specialty shops, franchised, 69-73, 146
    fraudulent practices of, 40-41
Springs, 117

Starter motor, 107, 108
Steering system, 81, 87, 118-120
Styling of cars, 10
Suing, 150-154
Suspension system, 81, 87, 115-118
Systems of automobile, 85-88

Tachometer, 94
Test drives. See Road tests
Thermostat, 99, 104, 130
Throttle valve, 99
Tie rods, 120
Timing gears, 94
Tires, 81, 134-135, 141
    frauds involving, 36-38
"Tool men," 38
Torque, 110-111, 115
Torus, 111-112
Towing, frauds involving, 43
Transmission, 87, 110-115
    automatic, 111-115
    frauds involving, 41-42, 43
    standard, 110-111
Transmission shops, 42, 71-72
Troubleshooting, 30
Tuneups, 136-137

Unitized construction, 87
Universal joints, 115
Used car warranties, 60

Valves, 93
Valve spring, 94
Venturi, 98-99
Voltage regulator, 105, 107
V-type arrangement of cylinders, 92

Warranty
    full, 58-59
    implied, 49, 58, 59, 60
    laws and, 57-61
    new-car, 13-14, 49-53, 56-57
Washing and waxing, 126-128
Water jackets, 101
Water pump, 101
Wheel alignment, 135-136
Winterizing a car, 138

1 Body (scratches)
2 Engine (quiet)
3 Exhaust (smoke, rust)
4 { Rust (interior, exterior)
    { Leaks
5 Tires
6 Belts
7 lights
8 Starter
9 Smooth rider
10 Miles
12 wear (seats, Break)   Accelerator
11 Year
13 Cost

Auto repair frauds
Norris, Monty

16730
629.28 NOR

629.28 Norris, Monty
NOR
        Auto repair frauds:
        how to prevent
        your car from
        driving you to the
        poorhouse

DATE			